GERMAN FOREIGN POLICY IN TRANSITION

The Royal Institute of International Affairs is an unofficial body which promotes the scientific study of international questions and does not express opinions of its own. The opinions expressed in this publication are the responsibility of the author.

The Institute gratefully acknowledges the comments and suggestions of the following who read the manuscript on behalf of the Research Committee: Alan Bullock, Roger Morgan, and Andrew Shonfield.

GERMAN FOREIGN POLICY IN TRANSITION

Bonn Between East and West

Karl Kaiser

*Issued under the joint auspices of the
Harvard University Center for International Affairs,
the Twentieth Century Fund's 'Tocqueville Series',
and the Royal Institute of International Affairs*

OXFORD UNIVERSITY PRESS

LONDON OXFORD NEW YORK

1968

Oxford University Press

LONDON OXFORD NEW YORK

GLASGOW TORONTO MELBOURNE WELLINGTON

CAPE TOWN SALISBURY IBADAN NAIROBI LUSAKA ADDIS ABABA

BOMBAY CALCUTTA MADRAS KARACHI LAHORE DACCA

KUALA LUMPUR HONG KONG TOKYO SINGAPORE

First published by Oxford University Press, London,
as an Oxford University Press paperback, 1968

PRINTED IN GREAT BRITAIN BY
BILLING & SONS LIMITED, GUILDFORD AND LONDON

TO DEBORAH

ABBREVIATIONS

CDU Christlich Demokratische Union (Christian Democrats)
CSU Christlich-Soziale Union (Christian Social Union –
     Bavarian wing of CDU)
FDP Freie Demokratische Partei (Free Democrats)
GDR German Democratic Republic
NPD Nazionaldemokratische Partei Deutschlands (National
     Democrats – extreme right)
SED Sozialistische Einheitspartei Deutschlands
     (Communist Party)
SPD Sozialdemokratische Partei Deutschlands (Social
     Democrats)

PREFACE

THIS manuscript grew out of the work on European and Atlantic affairs which I pursued in the stimulating and hospitable atmosphere of the Center for International Affairs at Harvard University. I would like to express my gratitude for its generous support to Robert Bowie, Thomas Schelling, and Raymond Vernon who directed it during my four-year stay there, and to Henry Kissinger who originally invited me to the Center. Their insight into international and European affairs helped me greatly in my work. I owe my greatest debt to Stanley Hoffmann; his friendship and encouragement made much of my work possible, and his ideas and scholarly achievements left a deep impression on my own thinking.

I am grateful to Ben Moore, director of the 'Tocqueville Series', established by him and others to associate Europeans and Americans in joint studies of their common problems. This group has since sponsored several successful conferences and books: the two first studies, by Pierre Hassner and John Newhouse, are listed in the bibliography of this essay. He encouraged me to proceed with this project and provided some of my support.

I am deeply indebted to the Royal Institute of International Affairs and Roger Morgan in particular, for their interest in this work and their contribution to its completion.

The final revision of the manuscript profited considerably from the brilliant reflections on the German problem which Richard Löwenthal presented at several seminar meetings of the German Research Program of Harvard University in March 1968. Besides the persons mentioned above, the following did me the invaluable service of reading and criticizing all or part of the manuscript: Karl Birnbaum, Karl Dietrich Bracher, and Hartmut Soell.

I am most grateful to the Deutsche Forschungsgemeinschaft which supported some of my work with a grant, and to Elizabeth Sifton and Bridget Martyn, both of whom edited the manuscript with skill, speed, and good humour. No debt, however, is as great as the one I owe to the person to whom the book is dedicated.

July 1968.   K.K.

CONTENTS

1

INTRODUCTION
A NEW TURN IN THE GERMAN PROBLEM?

FOR the first time since the Third Reich's total defeat more than two decades ago, Germany, or at least her western part, again seems about to become a major actor in international politics. West Germany's foreign policy is no longer entirely circumscribed by the will of her former occupying powers. This change occurs amid a general relaxation of the once rigid bipolar system that marked the years after World War II. Indeed, the erosion of bipolarity and West Germany's new self-assertion are inextricably interwoven. The division of Germany in the past has kept and will continue to keep the Federal Republic's margin of manoeuvre fairly narrow and has rendered every move precarious. In fact, Europe's future stability depends in part on how West Germany perceives this margin and how she exploits it. The 'German problem' thus appears in a new, more difficult, and more challenging per-spective—both for Germany herself and for international stability.

Why has the German problem taken a new turn? The answer lies in the changes that have occurred in the two major variables in the German equation: namely, the international system of the Cold War, which shaped the two German régimes, and the foreign and intra-German policies of the two German states. During the first two decades after the war these variables were arranged so as to produce a precarious but nevertheless effective stability. New developments have changed and rearranged them, and there is no certainty yet that a new equilibrium can be achieved.

Changes in the international system or in German policies have potentially far-reaching implications for Germany. This is so because of the unusually intensive interaction between domestic, intra-German, and international politics. The two German states are not régimes that created foreign policies, but foreign policies that created political régimes. Both emerged in a specific international constellation that deeply affected their political systems, constitutions, and ideologies, their party systems and internal political divisions. This was even more true for relations with the outside world since the Federal Republic's *raison d'être* was as closely linked to the West's then prevailing 'policy of strength' *vis-à-vis* the Communist world, of which it was both the instrument and outcome, as East Germany was to Stalin's desire to consolidate Russian control over eastern and central Europe and to use 'his' part of Germany as a basis for policies of expansion.

The domestic and foreign policies of the two German régimes were intricately connected with the international system and dialectically linked with each other, since, after all, the two states were still part of one common nation. The Cold War gave logic and coherence to this complex web, which endured various crises during two decades without breaking or leading to military conflict. (Given the odds against stability on this meeting-ground between two hostile systems, this was one of the truly remarkable features of the post-war period.)

The *détente* between East and West and the concomitant evolution of the bipolar system in the 1960s were therefore bound to have profound repercussions in Germany and on German policies. West Germany in particular was affected, since these developments called into question most of the essential tenets of her foreign and intra-German policies: her commitments to the Atlantic world, to the 'policy of strength' towards (and consequent isolation from) Eastern Europe and East Germany, to the Hallstein Doctrine (according to which Bonn would not maintain diplomatic relations with countries that gave diplomatic recognition to East Germany), or to a rejection of the Oder–Neisse line as the final German–Polish border. Simultaneously, the new international setting upset what was for the West Germans a delicate balance of gains and sacrifices in the form of support and promises by the West aimed at German unity on the one hand, and its (temporary) acceptance of the German division on the other.

In the early 1960s, then, the contradiction between the search for *détente* in the international world and West Germany's policies dating back to the early Cold War revealed the

Federal Republic as the last stronghold of orthodox policies of the past. But the dynamics of international evolution turned out to be irresistible, despite domestic opposition and mis-givings, and the West Germans began to revise their policy.

However, when West Germany fell into line with other Western policies of *détente* and changed her attitude towards Eastern Europe and the German Democratic Republic (GDR), none of those Western powers which had urged these changes upon her adequately realized that in so doing she was abandoning a set of policies which had been the basis of her past internal stability and a sense of purpose. Nor did they fully apprehend that the new course would expose West Germany to the very problems, challenges, and dangers from which, by imposing restrictions and encouraging almost the opposite policy, they had laboured to keep her sheltered in the past. Thus, as Henry Kissinger concisely stated, 'the current situation contains a series of time bombs'.[1]

It is no mere coincidence that the changes in German policies occurred immediately after the formation of the Great Coalition in December 1966. In fact, the double threat to West Germany's internal stability posed by the change in the international system and by the alteration in her foreign and intra-German policies made co-operation between the two main domestic political parties imperative, allowing in turn for new departures.

Today's international system can be represented as being one of what Stanley Hoffmann has aptly called 'muted bi-polarity', in which the East–West conflict continues to exist, but in muffled form.[2] Now Germany is a connecting link between East and West, since both German régimes fulfil two functions simultaneously. First, each comprises part of the meeting-ground between, and is an outpost of, the mutually opposing systems and could always tip the scale of Europe's stability—with Berlin as the most critical point. But secondly, together they form a *domestic context* with values and behaviour

---

[1] Henry A. Kissinger, *The Troubled Partnership; A Re-appraisal of the Atlantic Alliance* (1965), p. 209.

[2] Stanley Hoffmann, *Gulliver's Troubles, or the Setting of American Foreign Policy* (1968), p. 21.

patterns specific to such a situation and very different from those of relations between other members of the two political systems. Because of this double function as link and barrier, changes in German domestic or foreign policies are bound to affect the international system as a whole. This is true not only of changes effected in Germany by outside forces but also of developments generated within the two German régimes. Thus, for example, West German attempts to engage the East Germans in a dialogue, which began with the Social Democrats' abortive efforts to initiate a speakers' exchange in 1966, not only forced the Communist leadership of East Germany to reverse its intra-German policy, but also contributed to a severe strain in the GDR's relations with her socialist allies.

In the following essay I shall examine the changes in German policies, and the consequences arising from them. Four sets of questions will be kept in mind throughout the study. First, what changes have occurred in West Germany's policies on the division of the country, considered in the context of her foreign policy and of international politics after World War II? Second, what domestic and international factors contributed to this evolution? Third, what problems and dilemmas are raised by these developments, both for Germany and the Western powers? Finally, what patterns of interaction between domestic and international politics are characteristic of Germany, and what conclusions relevant to the peace and stability of Europe could be drawn from these observations?

I would emphasize that this study is not a history of German foreign policy of the post-war period, but only an essay. It deliberately focuses on certain themes and does not discuss in detail a number of dimensions, such as European integration, the evolution of the Western Alliance, or East European developments which a more complete study should include, some of which are covered by works listed in the bibliography (p. 140). Despite the emphasis of this study on the contemporary scene, it often places problems in a general international and historical context. Most important, many of the generalizations of this essay are hypothetical; they are intended to stimulate discussion, and obviously call for further verification and refinement.

In writing this study I have attempted to 'explore not just the assumptions and content of policy but also the environment from which policy develops and which influences and sustains it'.[3] This seems all the more necessary since I have examined aspects of a problem that has been conspicuously neglected as an object of systematic investigation, but that continues to be of vital importance to stability in the northern hemisphere.

[3] August Heckscher, in his introduction to the first paper in Pierre Hassner and John Newhouse, *Diplomacy in the West: Out from Paradox* (New York, 1966, mimeo; Tocqueville Series).

2

GERMANY AS A UNIFYING AND DIVISIVE FORCE IN INTERNATIONAL POLITICS

GERMANY has acted both as a unifying and a divisive force among the Western powers. Her drive for European hegemony twice forged a military and political alliance of unprecedented scope among the great powers and the host of smaller countries arrayed against her, whose interests in a number of other fields had hardly been in harmony.

In World War II the seriousness of the threat of the Axis and the global scope of its challenge called for unusual measures. And unusual measures were employed. One of them was Churchill's offer to France in 1940 to merge the two nations, citizenships, and parliaments. True, this was a last-ditch effort to back up a nation whose resistance was rapidly dissolving beneath the onslaught of the German armies, and it appeared as a mere historical curiosity shortly after it was made. But other measures had a more lasting effect. They ranged from the vast efforts to mobilize that part of the world economy not under Axis rule for the Allied war effort (Lend-Lease was only part of it) to what amounted to a unified Allied foreign and military policy. A number of ministries in various countries ceased to act within the national framework alone, and co-ordinated their activities with their Allied counterparts; common institutions and regular channels of communication were established not only militarily, where the armed forces were merged under common commands, but also in civilian life, in order to organize the economics and logistics of the war and to co-ordinate political and diplomatic aspects in connexion with the conflict and with planning for the future. Innumerable meetings took place on all levels, up to that of presidents and prime ministers, to co-ordinate action against Germany and her allies.

That this co-operation did not result in complete harmony is well documented in many studies, memoirs, and biographies. Numerous conflicts arose between Roosevelt, Churchill, Stalin, and de Gaulle, and they multiplied as the war drew to a close.

Not surprisingly, the patterns of co-operation and conflict emerged along geographical and historical lines that reflected identities or clashes of interests which far antedated the war. On certain issues a line could be drawn between Soviet Russia and the Western powers, while other lines divided—or united— the United States and Britain, though the Anglo-American relationship was no doubt the closest of them all. But whatever the differences and conflicts, the goal of defeating Germany and her allies was a powerful incentive for unity, to which all other considerations had to be subordinated. Many major disagreements were resolved through compromise or simply side-stepped so as not to endanger the common effort.

No wonder, then, that the unity of the Allied camp began to crumble when the defeat of the Third Reich was assured as only a matter of time. Once the German armies had surrendered, once Germany disappeared as an independent international actor and the victors had to make decisions affecting the future of Europe (on Germany's population, resources, and political organization), the compelling reasons for uniting into a common front receded. Instead, the historical experience and divergent interests of the powers involved increasingly affected their policies on Germany's future, their relations with one another, and the evolution of the European state system. Allied unity on German policy broke down as soon as Germany again became a stake in the international game and an area whose future was open.

Differences between the wartime Allies emerged not only between East and West but within the West as well. In fact, even before the East–West disagreements over Germany developed into an open break, the Western Allies were at variance about the future of the defeated country. These differences were reflected in the policies that Great Britain, France, and the United States pursued in their occupation zones and in the relations among them. On the issue of Germany's political structure, French demands for the nation's dismemberment into different states, British concepts favouring centralization, and American support of a federal solution clashed. The French obstruction to numerous measures proposed by the United States and Britain—the economic merger of the Western zones being one—paralysed effective co-operation almost as much as Soviet opposition did. American support of a free market economy conflicted with the inclination of some members of the Labour government of Britain to nationalize German industries. Compared to the Americans and British, the French were reluctant to grant the Germans administrative and political responsibilities. The list of policy differences could be continued. In particular, the clash of interests between France on one side and the British and Americans on the other thwarted many efforts to agree on the problems of Germany.

Unity of Western policy was restored only when the East–West confrontation removed, at least for the short run, the uncertainty about Germany's future by 'dividing the stake' through the establishment of two German régimes that were committed and closely tied to the goals and foreign policies of their respective camps. On the other hand, in the middle-term and long-term sense, Germany remained a stake and a problem: a stake because she was the object and the most valuable prize in the contest for Europe between East and West; a problem because whatever the outcome—continued division, re-unification along Communist, Western, or neutralist lines— the way it would affect Germany's internal texture and Europe's stability was uncertain and would have to be faced later. Moreover, the élites in both German régimes believed that the division was only temporary and that the eventual victory of their side would bring along with it an absorption of the other part of the country.

In any event, Western differences over what Germany's role would be in a future *all*-European state system seemed irrele-vant when East–West hostility and the division of the continent obviously blocked the emergence of such a system, and as long as Soviet power posed an acute military threat. Thus the West restored its unity of policy on Germany with the Cold War, and it did so by focusing on what amounted to establishing a role for *West* Germany in the *Western* system of states. Moreover, unity was achieved under American leadership and, for all practical purposes, through the accommodation of British and French policies to those of the United States.

Despite occasional disagreements, Western unity on the

German problem lasted until the beginning of the 1960s. The thaw in the Cold War, the efforts of America and Russia to sustain this thaw through various measures of *détente*, and the decreasing probability of military conflict in Europe eroded the earlier harmony. As the conflict became less acute and came to be seen as a transitory historical phenomenon, making the line of division through the continent appear more and more 'artificial', the older realities of Europe reasserted themselves. The unsolved questions of the past about the future of the European state system and the role of Germany in it could be and were raised again. Given the divergent national interests and views about Germany, Europe, and each nation in the future system, this too undermined Western unity over Germany.

Because of her resources and strategic position, Germany's policies and alignments are bound to affect the balance of forces in Europe. It is therefore all too natural that under sufficiently fluid circumstances every major power wants to influence Germany's course. By the early 1960s the two super-powers were no longer able to preserve their camps' unity on the German problem by imposing their own policies on the lesser powers. (Different policies pursued by France or Ru-mania are cases in point, and we shall return to them.) If any doubt remained that the Cold War had moved into an entirely new phase, the year 1967 should have removed it: for the first time since the world split into two hostile camps, *both* East and West were divided over the German problem. Thus a 'German syndrome' had come full circle again: as long as Germany was perceived as a threat she acted to encourage unity among the major powers; but she became a divisive force, as she had in the aftermath of World Wars I and II, the moment she began to become a stake and an area whose future was open.

But this lack of unity over Germany would have been less marked—indeed in the case of the East it would have been most unlikely—had there not been a volte-face both in Bonn *and* in East Berlin in 1966–7, a reversal that was at once a reflec-tion of and a further impetus to change in the Cold War. With this reversal, the Great Coalition government of Christian Democrats (CDU) and Social Democrats (SPD) in West

Germany swung round to a policy that a number of individuals within (and various groups outside) the earlier CDU government had advocated for some time without too much success, and whose adoption the Western allies had urged with growing insistence. Bonn abandoned the most important tenet of its 'policy of strength'—namely, that Germany's reunification was a prerequisite for any East–West *détente*—and accepted, instead, the argument that the best way to work for German unity was through a relaxation of East–West tension. This led to a revision of the Hallstein Doctrine and to an active *Ostpolitik* aiming towards West Germany's peaceful involvement in Eastern Europe. On the intra-German level, it resulted in a replacement of Bonn's uncompromising hostility towards East Germany with a selective policy of seeking contacts and co-operation short of diplomatic recognition.

In an almost complete reversal of roles, however, East Germany shunned the very contacts she had relentlessly professed to seek since her foundation. Abandoning her former strategy of reunification through intra-German recognition and confederation, she resorted to a position very similar to the 'policy of strength' that the Federal Republic was in the process of abandoning. Every West German effort to make contacts and work for a *détente* was now denounced (a stance similar to Bonn's reaction to East German probes at the height of the Cold War) as aggression in disguise or as a tactical ruse to pursue hidden imperialist goals.

Moreover, not unlike West Germany in the past, East Germany now tried to put pressure on her allies to support her orthodox position, when in reality some of them were interested in exploiting the opportunities that the thaw in East–West relations and the Federal Republic's 'peaceful offensive' in the East offered them. In fact, in order to thwart what he regarded as a dangerous outflanking manoeuvre by West Germany, the East German leader Walter Ulbricht even proclaimed 'a kind of Hallstein Doctrine in reverse' (though less radical than the original): Bonn's full recognition of East Germany now to be the prerequisite for its diplomatic relations with Communist countries.[4] Since the East German leaders did not cease to press

[4] Theo Sommer, 'Bonn Changes Course', *Foreign Affairs*, Apr. 1967, p. 489.

the issues, several East European allies on occasion could no longer hide their diverging points of view behind the convenient but increasingly ambivalent formulas of the past, and they chose open disagreement instead. Thus, the GDR's policy fostered disunity in the Communist camp.

By the mid-1960s a considerable gap had developed between the policies of the Federal Republic and those of her Western allies on the issues of German reunification and relations with the East. Clinging to the 'policy of strength', which sought a defeat of Communism through Western firmness, unity, ideological, economic, and military strength, Bonn had become an island of orthodoxy amidst Western attempts to alter policies towards the Communist world.[5]

But the difference in actual policy was also one in fundamental perspective. What to the Federal Republic was the upholding of a consistent policy which was inextricably tied to her very foundation, her internal structure, and the purpose of her foreign policy, which had been elaborated in co-operation with and partly at the insistence of the allies, was to the allies more and more an obstruction, if not a wilful sabotage, of their attempts to lower international tension. The Federal Republic's interest in 'keeping open' the problem of Germany's division and her ensuing refusal to accept the *status quo* were increasingly interpreted in the West (and, of course, in the East) as a threat to European stability, particularly in view of her implicit territorial demands and her steadily growing economic and military resources.

In the years 1964 and 1965 these fears, occasionally reinforced by Germanophobia, began to generate a tacit understanding among Western countries to ignore West Germany's doubts about the new policy of relaxation and to resist her demands, e.g. on the border issue. This understanding was epitomized in the argument, used increasingly during that period, that NATO, having been an instrument to resist the Soviet threat, was now also a means to contain a resurgent West Germany. But before such apprehensions were strong enough to restore the West's already foundering unity on the

---

[5] For a critical analysis of German policy in the latter part of 1965 see Karl Kaiser, 'Die deutsche Frage', *Frankfurter Hefte*, Nov. and Dec. 1965, Jan. 1966.

German problem, the Federal Republic in turn adopted the policy of furthering the *détente* and thereby inadvertently enabled the Western powers to reassert their divergent interests more forcefully. The change in German policy was visible in the first statements of the government formed by the Great Coalition, in particular the policy statement of Chancellor Kiesinger before the Bundestag on 13 December 1966 and Foreign Minister Brandt's declarations to NATO and WEU in the same month. Thus, both German régimes, in their own way and somewhat involuntarily, helped to foment international disunity over the German problem.

The Federal Republic's adoption of the prevailing Western course favouring *détente* raised at least as many problems as it solved. Several issues can be distinguished here: the threat to West Germany's internal stability as a result of her reorientation in foreign policy; the possibility of discord between the West and the Federal Republic; and, finally, the West's difficulties in dealing with these problems. We shall examine these questions in the following chapter.

3

THE WEST AND THE FEDERAL REPUBLIC: IMPLICATIONS OF CHANGE

THE Federal Republic was born of a unique conjunction of three forces: pressures from political groups within Germany; the occupation policies of the Western powers; and the imperatives of the Cold War. Combined, they produced a political system that owed its very existence to a then inescapable commitment to the West. As one leading scholar on German affairs has put it, 'The Federal Republic was born in 1949 as a twin sister of the Atlantic Alliance. Their father was the Cold War. It happened in 1949 and not 1945.'[6] But her *raison d'être* had two elements that represented two sides of the same coin: along with integration in Europe and the Atlantic world went the complete endorsement of a 'policy of strength' *vis-à-vis* the East which, in a way, meant West Germany's isolation until victory for the West. This policy framed her attitude towards the Communist world as a whole and towards her prime national problem: Germany's reunification was to be brought about through the collapse of Communism in East Germany—or the general breakdown of Communism in Eastern Europe.

The Federal Republic was established in 1949 as a non-sovereign state, but successive acts on the part of the Allies returned portions of sovereignty to the Germans, each time for a specific purpose, within clearly defined areas, and directing West German foreign activities exclusively to the West. Landmark revisions of the Occupation Statute and the gradual extension of sovereignty were therefore undertakings such as the European Coal and Steel Community, the (abortive) European Defence Community, and West Germany's admission to NATO and the Western European Union. Occasionally, as, for example, Secretary of State Dulles's support of Adenauer's CDU party in the German elections of 1953 showed, the Allies did not even shun intervention in West German domestic politics to secure the Federal Republic's involvement

[6] Alfred Grosser, *Die Bundesrepublik Deutschland; Bilanz einer Entwicklung* (1967), p. 12.

in the West. However, one critically important field was excluded from the transfer of sovereignty: all matters relating to Germany's basic national problem and West Germany's relations with the East. In the various treaties regulating the re-emergence of the Federal Republic as a 'sovereign' international actor, the Western powers reserved the right to make all decisions pertaining to the German division and Berlin.

Stability in the Bonn Republic

When West Germany embarks on a new course of involvement in Eastern Europe and takes a friendlier attitude towards the GDR, thereby (with considerable Western encouragement) breaking an established taboo, much more is at stake than a mere modification of foreign policy. Since the Federal Republic has been, so to speak, made to integrate with the West, to be isolated from the East—German or foreign—the new course directly affects the very foundation and fabric of her political system. Issues, patterns and terms of conflict in domestic politics, as well as the meaning and purpose of foreign policy are inevitably influenced.

The Western framework for domestic and foreign policy provided the Federal Republic with a fair degree of security and the possibility of becoming a respected member of the community of nations. These elements were crucial for a state whose self-confidence was precarious and whose relationship with the past was broken. But to a nation that always has had, and still has, a horror of being isolated, a weakening of this same framework, occurring simultaneously with internal and external pressure to set out on a new course, may be so severe a shock as to cause the domestic instability which the Western powers have always been eager to prevent. The destruction of the balance between promise and sacrifice, implied in the passage from a 'policy of strength' to a policy of *détente*, is an even more important generator of internal instability and discord with the Allies. And that leads to a second set of problems in Allied–German relations.

The Western 'policy of strength', while successful in its defensive goal of stopping Communist expansion in Europe, turned out to be illusory with regard to its offensive objectives, at least for those who believed its rhetoric. The Communist régimes in Europe did *not* collapse, and Germany remained divided. But whatever we may conclude now, with the benefit of hindsight, at that time this policy offered the Germans positive goals, consistency, and an acceptable balance between possible gains and sacrifices. The foundation of the Federal Republic, the simultaneous rehabilitation of West Germany, her economic recovery, and her growing sovereignty were linked with a renunciation of any immediate attempt to unify Germany and, hence, with a temporary acceptance of the division. But that acceptance was inscribed in an offensive strategy: the Federal Republic's integration in the West was part and parcel of a Western policy that held out the promise of reunification through free elections, a united democratic system, and a free market type of economy for the whole of Germany—in short, unity through a collapse of the East German régime (implying also a major defeat of international Communism).

The Western Allies rallied behind the Federal Republic's prime goal of national reunification from the moment the new state was established, and both agreed that substantial steps towards reunification were a prerequisite to a lasting *détente*. Allied support for this point of view was all the more necessary since the Western countries could not permit the Alliance to appear as an obstacle to unification at a time when they were eager to win the West Germans, who were internally divided over this very issue, to their side.

Thus the inherent contradiction between the Federal Republic's commitment to integration and alliance with the West on the one hand, and her national goal of unity on the other, was temporarily resolved by a quite explicit pledge from the Western powers to work towards reunification. Significantly, it was expressed most forcefully in the treaties and statements accompanying West Germany's accession to NATO in 1954-5.[7] The Allies' endorsement of West Germany's views on unity as a prerequisite to a *détente* seemed, to the Germans at least, to be

---

[7] See, e.g., the Declaration of the Three Western Powers of 3 Oct. 1954, at the London Conference, reprinted in B. Ruhm von Oppen, ed., *Documents on Germany under Occupation* (1955), p. 607.

part of a deal to reconcile them to the division by making it appear only temporary. The sacrifice was therefore compensated by two further assets in addition to the return of German self-respect, the establishment of a German state, international rehabilitation, and economic recovery: first, the Allied 'policy of strength', aimed *inter alia*, at German unity, and second, if no victory through strength were possible, a promise not to side-step the German issue when active East–West diplomacy was used to improve relations between the hostile blocs.[8]

The change to a policy of *détente* untied this 'package deal'. First, the 'policy of strength' was cast aside. Second, the principle that progress towards a relaxation of global tensions required progress on the German question was reversed: the relaxation of tension, to be sought in active East–West diplomacy and mutual involvement, would promote German unity. Hence the quasi-veto, which the earlier policy by implication conceded to the West Germans over Western efforts to achieve an East–West rapprochement, was thereby withdrawn. But even before this change occurred, bilateral efforts in East–West diplomacy, which Western states began to pursue, indicated that they were less and less willing to make progress towards global relaxation of tension dependent on the German problem which appeared insoluble for some time to come.

Third, West Germany's isolation from Eastern Europe implicit in the 'policy of strength' was abandoned. But this also meant forsaking the non-involvement in the Communist world, at once chosen and imposed, which had sheltered the young and vulnerable democratic régime from the potentially disruptive effect of dealing with the Communist world and from exposure to intra-German dialectics.

Fourth and lastly, the Western international structures, particularly those concerned with European integration, that had once offered Germany a new and meaningful place, so important in the absence of German unity and acting as an alternative to the traditional nation-state, entered a deepening crisis.

[8] For two perceptive analyses discussing the role of the German problem in Western diplomacy at different periods see works by Gerald Freund and Charles R. Planck, listed in the bibliography. For a more chronological treatment see Frederick H. Hartmann, *Germany between East and West* (1965).

What, then, was left of the 'package deal' of Western and German policy? First, what was supposed to be merely a transitory by-product—namely, the West German state—has assumed a high degree of permanency. What was intended to be a *Provisorium* has become a power with significant capabilities, the world's third industrial country and its second trading nation. Second, there remains the very condition which, so many Germans thought, the 'policy of strength' was designed to overcome: the division of Germany. In fact, it is deeper than ever, and two utterly different political and economic systems have emerged in the two parts of the country.

The abandonment of the 'policy of strength' was brought into sharp focus in a declaration of policy to the 1966 conference of the SPD by Helmut Schmidt, then its Deputy Parliamentary Leader:

The more these states [of the 'Free World'] are democratically structured, the more their leaders are dependent on their public opinion. And today that means that they depend on a public opinion which at present is only mildly interested in Germany's reunification. They depend on a public opinion in which for a long time, to say the least, fear of the risks involved in changing the status quo in Europe has been greater than a desire to see Germany reunified. In other words, the policy of strength has definitively and unequivocally failed.[9]

To the rest of the world, the abandonment of the 'policy of strength' signals a welcome relaxation of international tension which may open the way to a lasting peace in Europe. To the West Germans, however, it inevitably means failure of their previous policy on reunification, since it occurs at a time when the division appears fixed, with very little hope of change in the near future, whereas most of the policies that made that division temporarily acceptable have disappeared or changed. This difference in perspective could become the source of serious discord between Germany and her Western allies. As Henry Kissinger, a perceptive observer of Germany, has aptly pointed out, Germany's problems should be seen against the back-

[9] Helmut Schmidt, 'Deutschlandpolitik unter den sich ändernden weltpolitischen Bedingungen', speech delivered at the annual conference of the SPD, 3 June 1966, at Dortmund, *Tatsachen-Argumente* (publ. by the SPD), no. 205 (1966), p. 10.

ground of her deep sense of insecurity—particularly when we are dealing with failure or change in her most important policies, and with the part the Western allies took in their formulation. 'The German nightmare is a reappearance of the historical isolation that for almost its entire national history has forced Germany to confront hostility on all its borders, east and west. If this situation reappears, German worries could take dramatic forms. If the Federal Republic becomes the focal point of all European tensions, German frustrations are likely to turn on the seeming cause of its isolation.'[10]

Indeed, West German frustrations could conceivably result in a new version of an accusation of *Diktat*, charging the Allies with having forced on the Germans the partition of their country. The various elements involved in the temporary acceptance of the division would in this light be seen as cunning methods used to make the Germans accept the partition and keep the country divided. Time and again in the history of Europe other powers have stated that a weakened, divided Germany is in their interest. It would therefore not be too surprising if such a policy lent itself to this interpretation, which sees a purposive design where in fact—with the exception of France's efforts in the early post-war years—there was none. The momentum of history and of independent forces took the responsibility out of the hands of those who might have thought in those terms.

The myth of a *Diktat* and the accompanying accusations, so far mentioned only by extremists such as the National Democratic Party (NPD) and occasionally hinted at by moderates, would have disruptive consequences if they were to gain wider acceptance throughout the West German political spectrum. The myth would then only replace an older one which had a powerful effect in post-war Germany and which derived from the logic of the 'policy of strength'—arguing that the division of Germany was a result of the East–West conflict for which the East was *solely* responsible. Had not the Soviet Union consistently opposed reunification—on Western terms? In fact, it is hard to lay the blame for Germany's division at

[10] Henry A. Kissinger, 'For a New Atlantic Alliance' (text of a statement before the Senate Foreign Relations Cttee, 27 June 1966), the *Reporter*, 14 July 1966.

anybody's doorstep. With the exception of France, which for a time after the war consciously worked to dismember Germany, none of the wartime Allies had a clear conception of the future of Germany—not even the Soviet Union, contrary to established opinion. As Hans-Peter Schwarz has shown so well, the division resulted from the conjunction of: (1), specific measures taken by the occupying powers, trying to postpone the ultimate decisions about Germany but in fact setting the stage for the division; (2), a specific constellation of domestic political forces in the two parts of Germany; and (3), the gradual polarization of the existing East–West rivalries in a conflict on German soil.[11]

The changes in Western policies towards the Communist world therefore mean different things to the Western powers and to the West Germans. As Raymond Aron perceptively put it, 'The basic cause of the present German crisis is this: all the West seems, in German eyes, too ready to accept the partition of Germany. It is no longer a question whether unification must precede or follow *détente*, but whether the *détente* will lead to German reunification or to the maintenance of the two States.'[12]

To sum up, growing certainty about continued division undermines the Federal Republic's *Selbstverständnis*: her self-perception and sense of purpose. Her leaders, as Richard Löwenthal has rightly pointed out, deliberately abstained from creating a loyalty in her citizens towards the state.[13] Strictly speaking, they did not even become citizens but were merely Germans living there, whose real loyalty was supposed to be divided between two entities still to be created, namely a united Europe and a united Germany.

With both prospects dampened or destroyed, the political system finds itself in a spiritual void which makes it more vulnerable to internal and external challenges and which forces it into a painful process of adaptation and redefinition of its purpose. Both processes are inextricably intertwined with West Germany's Eastern policy, to which we shall now turn.

[11] See Schwarz, *Vom Reich zur Bundesrepublik* (1966). See also Peter H. Merkl, *The Origins of the West German Republic* (1963).

[12] Raymond Aron, 'Is the European Idea Dying?', *Atlantic Community Quarterly*, Spring 1967, p. 43.

[13] Richard Löwenthal, 'Problems of Contemporary Germany' (provisional title), Mar. 1968, forthcoming.

Lifting a taboo: how to face the East

Trouble may arise in Germany's relations with the West not only as a result of frustration and resentment. One of the reasons (among several others) why the Allies restricted the sovereignty of the young Federal Republic by reserving for themselves ultimate decision on all matters relating to reunification and Berlin was, as we have seen, to protect her from danger. West Germany's present interest in more direct contact with the East exposes her to the very challenges and dangers they had in mind.

With the Cold War the dominant factor in European and world politics, it was the Western powers' overriding concern to secure a Western orientation of the new German state west of the Elbe. The policies deriving from this concern (which, incidentally, also reflected a growing consensus in West German society) had several goals. Three are particularly important. First, there was the immediate objective of enlisting West German co-operation and of mobilizing her resources to aid in the struggle against the Communist powers. Second and more important, this Western outpost, in the late 1940s only a nascent democracy, had to be protected from internal and external threats and challenges of Communism, all the more real since Communism reigned in the other part of Germany. Third and most important, the efforts of both West German leaders and the Western Powers to commit West Germany firmly to the West were intended to alleviate, if not to eliminate, the consequences of Germany's historical position as a *Land der Mitte* (land of the middle). This pivotal position between East and West, fraught with uncertainties, temptations, and dangers, had been at the root of Germany's sense of insecurity, her frequent isolation, and her quest for identity. Europe as a whole had several times suffered from the tragic consequences. Direct dealings between the Federal Republic and the East were therefore avoided after the Cold War broke out. Moreover, by ensuring complete Allied supervision of relations with the East and by retaining ultimate power of decision, the Federal Republic was effectively sheltered both from its threats and temptations.

The policy of non-involvement with the East and full integration in the West, as it was pursued by Konrad Adenauer with ironclad tenacity and with the full support of the Western Allies, attempted to deal with 'the German problem' at its most essential level. A firm, if possible irreversible, commitment to an integrated structure in the West was to change the basic elements of the German equation by denying Germany her historic 'middle position', and to relegate her to the periphery and frontier of the Western system.[14] It was hoped that this would prevent the recurrence of both the German nationalism and the the ill-fated 'seesaw policies' of the past.

The irony of recent and current Western attempts to press or induce the Federal Republic to 'turn to the East' is now that they create the very dangers of a 'middle position' from which earlier policies tried to protect her. But given the fact that, despite two decades of division, Germany is still one nation, that, furthermore, the line of Europe's partition runs right through her territory, and that, finally, she occupies a crucial political position in the heart of the Continent, any meaningful solution to Europe's division and any rapprochment between the two sides must by necessity include Germany. So the present policy of *détente* in Europe is bound to raise a number of the historical problems inherent in Germany's geographical position on the Continent.

It is all too evident that Western calls for a more active engagement in Eastern Europe have affected the foreign policy of the Federal Republic. We shall examine this transition in greater detail later. Its outline may suffice here to bring into relief some of the problems raised by these changes. The Great Coalition of December 1966 by no means initiated the new approach; the groundwork had been laid under Foreign Minister Gerhard Schröder in the early 1960s. Then, trade missions were established in several Communist countries, but further measures, let alone a general revision of policy towards the East, were blocked by opposition within the CDU—CSU, control of which was gradually slipping out of Chancellor Erhard's hands.

---

[14] On this aspect see Klaus Erdmenger, *Das folgenschwere Missverständnis; Bonn und die sowjetische Deutschlandpolitik 1949–55* (1967); Werner Feld, *Reunification and West German-Soviet Relations* (1963); and James L. Richardson, *Germany and the Atlantic Alliance* (1966), pp. 11–62.

B

Only the Great Coalition with the SPD gave a clear majority to those who were eager to have a different policy towards the East.

In addition to abandoning the old hostility to the GDR and adopting a more conciliatory attitude on the border problems, West Germany revised her endorsement of the Hallstein Doctrine. Bonn accepted relations with the East European countries since, it was now held, they had had no choice but to recognize East Germany during Stalin's rule. In January 1967 diplomatic relations were established with Rumania, in January 1968 with Yugoslavia. Similar attempts with other Communist countries have, despite initial progress in some cases, been stalled by the counter-offensive which the Soviet Union and East Germany launched in 1966.

The desire for diplomatic relations with Eastern Europe is only one aspect of the more fundamental and profound desire to revise West Germany's relationship with the East. Evidence has steadily increased in public debates, in a growing stream of statements, articles, and books, and it has spread—sometimes with surprising swiftness—to groups and forces that were once the advocates of an uncompromising attitude towards the Communist world. The breadth and frequently the radicalism of many of the proposals—ranging from a call for independent West German action in the East[15] or advocacy of an alliance with Communist China,[16] to more qualified proposals for an *Öffnung nach Osten* (opening to the East)[17] in co-operation with the West—reveal several important factors. First, West Germany's renewed interest is by no means *only* a reaction to the Western powers, but draws on native aspirations. Some of these are older than the West's efforts to achieve *détente* and are activated by the same forces that in the late 1940s and early 1950s supported a 'third way'—or neutrality—between East and West; other persons advocating change, while being

[15] This has been on the whole the line taken by the influential magazine *Der Spiegel;* see in particular Rudolf Augstein, 'Für ein neues Rapallo?', 25 Apr. 1966.

[16] Hans-Georg von Studnitz, *Bismarck in Bonn: Bemerkungen zur Aussenpolitik* (1964).

[17] Title of a book by Paul Sethe (Frankfurt, 1966); for other critical analyses see works by Peter Bender, Eberhard Schulz, Wilhelm Wolfgang Schütz, and Theo Sommer, listed in bibliography.

firmly oriented to the West, simply drew their own conclusions from the failure of the 'policy of strength'. Second, these radical and far-reaching proposals reveal a measure of disenchantment with the West. And third, they reveal that the historical uncertainties about Germany's 'middle position' in Europe linger on. The search for Germany's identity and her place on the continent has simply taken a new turn. The forces that sought a peaceful *modus vivendi* with the East, after being silent, powerless, or frustrated for a decade, have been given the opportunity to reassert themselves.

These forces may however not necessarily threaten stability in Central Europe or in Allied–German relations. After all, West Germany could not have remained the last stronghold of Cold War postures for ever. But, as Stanley Hoffmann has rightly observed in his incisive study of American–European relations, a 'new emphasis on results', which sharply contrasts with the declaratory character of the earlier 'policy of strength', considerably magnifies the dangers in West Germany's 'opening to the East'.[18]

A policy of involvement in the East that replaces waiting with activism, and resignation to a temporarily inflexible situation with a belief in real opportunities for progress, is particularly vulnerable to failure. A setback of policy that under earlier circumstances could be seen as the product of an impossible situation now becomes clear defeat. Moreover, failure seems probable as long as the Soviet Union has little interest in any change except one that would consolidate the *status quo* or modify it to her advantage. If the 'policy of movement' leads to little more than 'consecrating the division of Europe at a lower level of hostility',[19] West Germany's political leaders may well put the blame for the failure, not on the intractability of the problem, but on the Western Allies. And, in truth, the Western powers might have to share some of the blame. As students of German politics have pointed out repeatedly,[20] the Federal Republic has been under pressure

[18] Hoffmann, *Gulliver's Troubles*, p. 432.

[19] Ibid., p. 434.

[20] See, e.g., Kissinger, *The Troubled Partnership*, and his Senate Testimony of 1966, 'For a New Atlantic Alliance', *The Reporter*, 14 July 1966, p. 4.

from the Western powers to enact irreconcilable policies with regard to her dealings with the Communist world. And as a country whose sense of insecurity is considerable and whose sense of identity is problematic, the combined strain of conflicting pressures from allies and of frustration from failure may seriously threaten domestic stability in Germany.

A new *Ostpolitik* that maintains territorial claims and subtly tries to undermine Soviet influence may appear too threatening to the Russians or to Eastern Europe to be successful, yet too active not to revive fears in the West of a new Rapallo. The worst that could happen would be the increasing isolation of the Federal Republic. This, together with uncertainty about Germany's future domestic stability, would significantly weaken the Western Alliance. To what extent it would invite new diplomatic offensives from the Soviet Union can only be guessed. Past Soviet pronouncements suggest that the Soviet leaders are aware of the untested potential of more friendly and compromising approaches towards the Germans, and merely to test these strategies could seriously challenge European stability.

To be sure, the current implementation of West Germany's new *Ostpolitik* leaves little doubt about Bonn's firm commitment to the West, its values and its institutions. It is a far cry from an updated version of the famed 'seesaw policy', about which suspicious as well as understanding observers of Germany have begun to warn again. Whether one studies past pronouncements of former Foreign Minister Gerhard Schröder or more recent statements by those leaders of the Great Coalition who have prominently shaped the terms of the new foreign policy, attachment to the West unquestionably has priority. They have defined the tasks stemming from Germany's central position in Europe as follows: 'For centuries Germany formed a bridge between Western and Eastern Europe. We intend to rebuild that broken bridge.'[21] Their statements put the main emphasis on attachment to Western institutions and to friendship with the United States and France, as well as on European

---

[21] Willy Brandt, to the Council of Europe, Strasbourg, 24 Jan. 1967. For an almost identical statement by Chancellor Kiesinger see the Government Declaration of 13 Dec. 1966, reprinted in *Bulletin*, Press and Information Agency of the Federal Government, 14 Dec. 1966.

unification. Similarly, rarely do the Coalition's statements on foreign policy neglect the opportunity to warn against illusions about immediate or spectacular results, or to point to West Germany's precariously narrow margin of manoeuvre and the absolute necessity for the support of (and German co-operation with) the Western Allies.

In the past West Germany has dealt with the East in two different ways: by a policy of certainty, acting as a bulwark of the West, and by a policy of uncertainty, dealing with East and West in a seesaw fashion. As a model for the future, both are ruled out by the lessons of European history and experience as untenable and undesirable. To maintain the Federal Republic as a Western bulwark, co-operative towards the West and defensive towards the East, presupposes a division of Europe into two hostile camps. Everybody wants to overcome this, or at least professes to. It also implies continued isolation from the East and abandonment of the idea of a single German nation, and the West Germans are unlikely to accept either. Finally, if the Federal Republic were kept as a Western bulwark, rapprochement between East and West would have to exclude and bypass Europe's crucial centre— an altogether untenable position if the rapprochement is intended to be permanent.

Nor is there any desire to revive the 'seesaw policy' between East and West. Apart from the fact that it will remain impossible as long as East–West antagonism does not diminish, the memories of its earlier disastrous consequences for Germany and for Europe, to which two wars testify, are still powerful. Any attempt to revive it would meet with overwhelming opposition in the West as well as among responsible German leaders.

There may, however, be a third way, sometimes advocated in the West, notably by President de Gaulle. Such a strategy would attempt to overcome Germany's division through a long-run process of relaxation of tensions and a rapprochement between East and West Europe to which Germany could make an important contribution. This would reconcile the necessity for a basically Western orientation of the Federal Republic with the fulfilment of tasks and opportunities stemming from Germany's geographically central position; at the same time, it might reconcile two policy needs which have in the past seemed mutually exclusive—namely, stability in Europe and the overcoming of Europe's and Germany's division.

A policy assigning to West Germany a constructive role in alleviating the East–West conflict and resolving the division of Germany, without severing her essential ties with the West, appears to be in the making, and no doubt it will lead to a more active West German role in European affairs. As the SPD put it in a resolution of its 1968 party conference: 'To us, Eastern and Western policy are no alternatives. *Ostpolitik* requires backing from as well as co-operation and co-ordination within the West. Constructive *Ostpolitik* also increases the weight of the Federal Republic in the West. Both [policies] are equally important, both serve all of Europe.'[22]

The international environment, as we shall see, now offers more favourable conditions for such a new course than in the past, and within West Germany the changes already discussed point in this direction. The different attitude is also manifest in the West Germans' exploration of new ideas, willingness to make compromises, and discussion about new security arrangements that include both East and West.

In fact, there is little doubt that West German policy has already been drastically modified. The abandonment of the 'policy of strength' made the West Germans face up to the fact that it had failed on the issue that had been most important to them—namely, the division of their country. From this realization it was a swift step to a policy of experimentation *vis-à-vis* East Germany, in order to make up as soon as possible for more than fifteen years of mutual hostility, isolation, and separation, to save what could be saved. After several years of reassessment in the 1960s, the crucial stage was entered when, in the spring and summer of 1966, the SPD proposed to the East German Communists an exchange of prominent party figures who would speak in the other half of the country. After initial acceptance, East Berlin turned the offer down, probably because the régime felt it would not fulfil its own expectations and lead to unrest in the East German population.

[22] *Parteitag der Sozialdemokratischen Partei Deutschlands 1968*, p. 996.

Later on, in December 1966, with the formation of the Coalition Government, a policy of contacts was adopted officially. It quickly led, by April 1967, to the unprecedented step of the West German Chancellor and the SPD sending messages to the East German Communist Party Congress in which they outlined specific proposals for intra-German contacts. And by the summer of 1967 Chancellor Kiesinger and the East German Premier Stoph were engaging in an exchange of notes. While the details of this evolution will be scrutinized further below, one aspect of West German policy must be mentioned in this context: namely its ambiguity. Contacts were the order of the day, but would they not help to consolidate and deepen the German division?

To the East German leaders, the 1966 episode of the speakers' exchange probably suggested that if Bonn took up the policy of contacts which they themselves had professed to seek for more than a decade, the fabric of the East German polity would be exposed to dangers that could seriously weaken the Communist régime. Out of this realization grew the reversal in their policy to which we have already alluded. For all practical purposes, Ulbricht prohibited low-level contacts between the two parts of Germany by posing new conditions for negotiations, notably that the working class must first come to power in West Germany and that negotiations could only begin subject to prior recognition of the GDR by the Federal Republic.

Given the ambiguity of the Federal Republic's policy towards the GDR and Ulbricht's efforts to channel them into a recognition of his régime, the possibility of failure is a real one (though much depends, of course, on how the West German leaders define success). Since it is less the actual failure that matters than the consequences of frustration, the new policy towards East Germany could generate strains on, if not disruption of, West German domestic politics. Moreover, only the future will show whether West Germany's old policy, firmly committed to the West, has sufficiently changed the fundamental elements of the German equation to permit her to enter this new phase of active Eastern involvement without rocking European stability.

Whatever the hopeful prospects, the dilemmas and dangers

remain. And they are complicated and aggravated by the interaction between intra-German relations and international politics. The scope of this essay does not permit a detailed examination of this point, but a few observations are relevant to our analysis.

The two German régimes, as was suggested earlier, perform a dual role. On the one hand, they are the meeting-place and respective outposts of two hostile international systems. As such, they could tip the scales of Europe's stability. On the other hand, they are two parts of one nation and, therefore, taken together, form a *domestic* national context with its own habits of thought and action, quite different from those characteristic of relations between other nations in opposing international systems.

What follows from this duality? First, the division of Germany acts as a potential 'escalator' for international problems. Important international issues or disagreements, once entangled in the dialectics of intra-German relations, assume a different character in the domestic context—usually a more threatening one, since *each* régime suffers from its own version of a deep sense of insecurity. And since the structure of *both* polities have been shaped decisively by a specific international constellation that is now undergoing a transformation, both régimes have become hyper-sensitive to the 'domestic', intra-German consequences of change in the environment. This state of affairs assures the working of the 'escalator' mechanism. Thus, an East–West *détente* can mean to Bonn confirmation of the *status quo* as well as a challenge to its claim to speak for all Germany; to East Berlin it could imply that the GDR is becoming less essential to the Socialist camp; to both, it can represent a threat in one way or another.

Since both German régimes play such a crucial role in the international system, any problem, once fed into the workings of intra-German dialectics, becomes magnified. For this reason, the German escalating syndrome often dampens or blocks movement in the international environment. As the history of the nuclear Test-Ban Treaty shows, an East German signature on an international arms-control agreement challenged the Federal Republic's claim to represent all Germany, creating one further problem on an issue that already bristled with them. Similarly, diplomatic relations between Communist nations and West Germany have been—and are—perceived in East Berlin as a threat to weaken its position *vis-à-vis* the Federal Republic.

In addition to acting as an 'escalator', the German division tends to *externalize* domestic problems. Since it is on German soil that the two opposing international systems meet, overlap, and, so to speak, interpenetrate, a wide range of domestic problems in the two polities immediately concern the international environment. Events within as well as between the two German régimes can bear directly on the stability of Europe—be they the rise of a right-wing party in the West, a change in the East German leadership, or attempts by East and West German leaders to make contact.

For these reasons the German division appears to some people as an ever-present problem that might trigger off unexpected discord in a world willing to settle with the *status quo*; to others it represents a notorious obstacle to movement and necessary change. How, then, do the dynamics of the German division with their syndromes of 'escalation' and 'externalization' affect relations between the Western powers and Germany? Whether change and movement in intra-German relations are potentially disruptive to both polities or whether they would lead to progress (if by that we mean lowering the level of hostility and alleviating the inhuman consequences of the division), the Western powers have an interest and a stake in the outcome of intra-German initiatives.

Difficulties for Western action

The Western powers may try to postpone a settlement of the German problem, if not to alleviate some of its consequences, but whatever they do, they can never entirely escape it. They are free to encourage West Germany to take initiatives of her own, but if failure comes, it will always be the West as a whole that will have to share the burden of it. Hence the West, out of enlightened self-interest as much as because of previous commitments, has to assume a major share of the responsibility for future developments in central Europe. But several important difficulties hinder wise and effective action.

First, to understand the complexity of the problems involved, let alone to elaborate strategies to deal with them, requires a major and continuous effort. Moreover, the hidden dynamics and inbuilt escalator mechanisms in a divided Germany call for an awareness of the urgency of the problems involved; this cannot be easily manufactured and is often in short supply.

Second, the scope of the tasks ahead makes it difficult to create effective and far-sighted strategies. The West faces a series of dilemmas. It has to encourage the Federal Republic's involvement in the East so that a rapprochement between East and West can comprise the whole of Europe. Yet care must be taken that this does not lead to West Germany's isolation or the exploitation of her weakness by the Soviet Union. That is to say, West Germany's links with the West must be preserved without impeding her indispensable contribution to a *détente*. Moreover, Western intervention may frequently be imperative, but the costs of heavy-handed imposition will be high. A healthy aloofness from the affairs of Europe, in particular on the part of the United States, will often be desirable, but if this is reduced to passive waiting, control over an inherently dynamic issue will slip out of hand.

The problem is magnified by the concerns that two of the Western powers have in other parts of the world commanding their attention and energies. America struggles with the intractable war in Vietnam, and Britain must cope with commitments overseas and a difficult economic situation at home. Since these other issues conflict with the priority given to, and necessity for, both the dialogue with the Soviet Union and *détente* in general, they create impatience and encourage ill-advised shortcuts through the tangle of Germany's and Europe's problems. (Nor is this careful study facilitated by the phobic ambivalence intermittently characteristic of British attitudes towards Germany.) Among the Western powers, only France gives unequivocal priority to the problems of Europe and its division. But her policies are at variance with those of her allies, and this leads to the second difficulty in dealing with Germany: disunity in the West.

Barring unforeseen events that would draw the Western Allies together again, it seems impossible to reach an agreement on the basic issues, except one that represents a mere congruence on general principles as the lowest common denominator, too general to be of use in preventing minor difficulties from becoming major disruptive imbalances. The same *détente* that requires co-ordination of the new problems it creates in the two parts of Europe, simultaneously renders such co-operation more difficult, since it has enabled each nation to act again according to its more traditional but also more divergent interests. In this respect, both East and West face similar problems. In fact, in their differences over Germany, the two camps appear to reinforce each other by following what Pierre Hassner has called a 'symmetry postulate'.[23]

Finally, with regard to Germany, the West, like the East, has memories of the past. The fact that these are less operative among Western powers than among Eastern ones, which have gone out of their way to keep alive the past as a means to garner support from a varied population, is balanced somewhat by the Western democracies' responsiveness to feelings and actions of the populace motivated by historical memories. The specific attitudes of other countries on issues related to Germany—ranging from West German policies on Germany's borders or on nuclear weapons, to the prospect of a merger of the two parts of Germany—can be understood only in the context of their particular historical consciousness. This closely and intensely associates a united, powerful Germany with a challenge to their own position, if not existence. Memories of the cataclysmic experience of World War II and the sufferings endured under German occupation sustain this mental connexion.

Undoubtedly there are other West European countries besides Germany where nationalism and a weak democratic process have been marked. But when such characteristics occur in modern Germany, they assume special importance since they buttress the historical association between a strong or united Germany on the one hand and a threat to the rest

[23] Pierre Hassner, 'German and European Unification: Two Problems or One?', *Survey*, Oct. 1966, pp. 14–37.

of Europe on the other. It is in this context that one must view the reservations of other nations, whether Communist or Western, about the future of German democracy, reservations that almost two decades of relatively well-functioning Bonn democracy have been unable to dissipate. A number of incidents in the Federal Republic—the appointment of men considered as former Nazis to high posts, and occasional examples of official disregard for civil liberties—kept alive old fears. Similarly, the modern forms of moderate German nationalism, whose resurgence has been encouraged by all major political parties since the early 1960s, has paradoxically strengthened, in the wake of increased pressure for reunification, resistance to German unity and suspicion of Germans *per se*. This is even more true of the revival of the extreme right wing in West Germany, as manifested by the electoral successes of the NPD in the mid-1960s, and of some West German reactions to the projected non-proliferation treaty on nuclear weapons. Both are complex phenomena which can be easily overestimated or misinterpreted, but—partly because of this fact—they reactivated or confirmed historical memories and fears at the very time when the Bonn government was seriously trying to shelve the legacy of the Cold War and engage in a new policy of *détente*.

But the essential motive in the formation of a historical consciousness, as Arnold Bergstraesser has pointed out, lies in one's concern for the future.[24] In drawing conclusions from the past to serve as guides for the future, one normally uses historical evidence and experience in the light of preconceived objectives. Thus, if it is correct that other European nations closely associate a strong or united Germany with a threat to their existence, this might well imply that their guide for the future will be to prevent the re-emergence of such a Germany. If this is even only partially true, a German policy of reunification must overcome very deep-rooted obstacles. Of course, a more positive attitude on German unity is not impossible—every development remains within the realm of possibility if

[24] Arnold Bergstraesser, 'Geschichtliches Bewusstsein und politische Entscheidung', in Waldemar Besson, ed., *Geschichte und Gegenwartsbewusstsein: Festschrift für Hans Rothfels* (1963).

we believe that it is the human will that shapes the course of history—but the resistance to change differs from and is stronger than that which the West German view on reunification, and on a more important place for Germany in European politics, has often suggested.

4

THE PROBLEM OF THE GERMAN BORDERS

AMONG the problems most influenced by historical memories the unsettled questions of Germany's borders are paramount. The two cataclysmic wars of the twentieth century and earlier wars are too closely associated, in European minds, with territorial disputes to prevent the unsolved issues of Germany's eastern borders being viewed as a potential threat to European stability. On both border problems—the Oder–Neisse frontier between Poland and East Germany (including the ceding of parts of East Prussia to the Soviet Union) and the fate of the Sudeten part of Czechoslovakia—the position of the Western powers is crucially important. This is not so much because some of them were parties to the treaties that bore upon these matters (those of Munich in 1938 and of Potsdam in 1945) as because these powers had a major effect on the evolution of these problems in the past and will continue to have in the future.

The evolution of Germany's border policy

The Federal Republic inherited the frontier problems as part of the legacy of the Third Reich and its defeat. In complete accord with the policies of the Western Allies in the years of the Cold War, West Germany rejected the territorial *status quo*. Supported in this by her allies for more than a decade, she has consistently refused to accept the Oder–Neisse line as the permanent Polish-German border and has insisted on negotiating the eastern frontier of a reunited Germany only in a final peace conference. Although the determination not to weaken Germany's bargaining position blurred the conciliatory elements that actually existed in the West German point of view, official West German policy has been fairly rigid.[25]

[25] For an analysis of the Oder–Neisse question in German foreign policy of the first decade, which recognizes the importance of these territories to Poland, see Georg Bluhm, *Die Oder-Neisse-Linie in der deutschen Aussenpolitik* (1963); Golo Mann, *Verzicht oder Forderung? Die deutschen Ostgrenzen* (1964); Hansjakob Stehle, *Nachbar Polen* (1963).

West Germany's policy on the eastern frontiers led many East Europeans, and even some sections of public opinion in the West, to depict the Federal Republic either as a *revanchist* country or—in less offensive terms—as an 'anti-*status-quo* power'. When West German officials spoke of a *deutscher Rechtsanspruch* (German legal claim) to the territories east of the Oder–Neisse, both East and West tended to overlook the legality of such a position and saw in it, instead, an indication that a reunited Germany would demand territories from present European states. Other policies reinforced this interpretation. The Federal Republic did—and still does—claim the principle of self-determination for the German people as a whole. For the many Germans expelled from former German territories or from the Sudeten part of Czechoslovakia (today they form about 15 per cent of the West German population), she demanded the *Recht auf Heimat* (right to the homeland) which she more or less unilaterally raised to the status of a 'basic right of international law'.[26] While the policy undoubtedly contained room for compromise in ultimate negotiations, Eastern and Western countries tended to interpret these two demands as formulas enabling the Germans to return to Soviet, Polish, and Czech territories and then, in pursuance of self-determination, to vote for their reincorporation into Germany.

The fact that a rising number of voices within Germany criticized these official policies did not dissipate fears in Eastern Europe and apprehension in the West, so long as the Bonn government was unwilling to recognize the existing border. Similarly, the official disavowal of any claims to Czechoslovak territory failed to become credible because of a simultaneous refusal (which only the Great Coalition of 1966 reversed) to declare the Munich Agreement legally invalid. To the East Europeans, upholding the agreement seemed to imply that the German–Czech border could still be changed in indirect ways—e.g. through the repatriation of Sudeten Germans who might then press for a special territorial status or a return to Germany.

[26] For the claim that the 'right to the homeland' has become an internationally accepted principle, comparable with the principle of self-determination, see 'Das Menschenrecht auf Heimat', *Bulletin*, 23 Dec. 1964. For a critique see Hans A. Stöcker, 'Völkerrechtliche Implikationen des Heimatrechts', *Europa-Archiv*, Aug. 1966, pp. 547–54.

The fact that Chancellor Erhard, despite internal opposition, retained Hans-Christoph Seebohm in his cabinet after the elections of 1965 confirmed these apprehensions, for Seebohm, as a leader of the Sudeten Germans, was particularly adamant on the 'right to the homeland' and the continued validity of the Munich Agreement.

Because of the more or less uncompromising manner in which the Federal Republic saw fit to reject the existing boundaries during the first fifteen years of its existence, its repeated renunciations of the use of force in connexion with these territorial questions were simply not taken at face value. Conciliatory elements in West Germany were lost out of sight when stern refusal followed even moderate domestic proposals, such as the one to 'talk' with the Poles about the frontiers.[27] The official (and therefore binding) territorial claims frequently voiced in public by cabinet ministers contributed to the suspicions with which the German claims were received by other nations. Moreover, the new economic and military strength of the Federal Republic began to work against her, for the East European leaders appeared to believe that Bonn would in some way actually use her existing capabilities to pursue declared interests.

Nevertheless, during the Cold War, West Germany had full support for her official position from all her Western allies. In fact, their policy on the border issues was one of their contributions to the 'package deal' accompanying the formation of the Federal Republic, and it helped to enlist and sustain active West German support for both the 'policy of strength' and the temporary acceptance of the division of Germany. As the years passed, it became clearer that any attempt to change the territorial *status quo* would upset the precarious balance in Europe. And with the thaw in East–West relations, Western endorsement of Bonn's position was given with growing uneasiness. Public opinion began to regard the existing borders as permanent. But the governments continued to support their German ally, assuming that their relations with the Federal Republic would only be strained if they were to state publicly that a real-

[27] Such a proposal was made by Fritz Erler, late Vice-Chairman of the SPD. *Die Welt*, 16, 18 and 30 Jan. 1965.

istic policy on German reunification required major territorial concessions, if not recognition of the Oder–Neisse line.

President de Gaulle deviated from this general pattern when in 1959 he recognized Poland's western border as the final frontier for a reunited Germany, a position which he forcefully restated during his visit to Poland in September 1967. Though his action had the long-term effect of aiding the process of reappraisal in West Germany, it did not induce other Western powers to follow suit. On the contrary, the deepening antagonism between the United States and the Fifth Republic, and their competition for the loyalty of West Germany, induced Washington to use uncompromising support of the West German position as one of the means to elicit Bonn's friendship.[28]

By the mid-1960s, however, the growing Western consensus that West German concessions on the frontier questions would be desirable became evident in official pronouncements. Though none approached de Gaulle's position, they began to move in that direction. For example, Secretary of State Dean Rusk's remark at the end of 1964 that prior to negotiations on German reunification the Federal Republic and the West would have to clarify their views both on the military status and on the territorial problem, was interpreted as an expression of that line of thinking in the United States which was in increasing disagreement with Bonn's orthodoxy.[29] Britain's mass media, and, privately, her political élites, have also disagreed with Bonn's frontier policy since the late 1950s, but official policy, if called to give an opinion, always tersely endorsed West Germany's legal position that a final settlement could only be achieved at a peace conference. A change of official policy was indicated by the then Foreign Secretary George Brown's remark that 'in a way' the Anglo-Soviet communiqué following discussions with Premier Kosygin in February 1967 implied British recognition of the Oder–Neisse line. (The Anglo-Soviet communiqué had mentioned 'respect for the

[28] See, e.g., the State Department declaration on the Oder–Neisse line, issued after Soviet Foreign Minister Gromyko reported an alleged Franco-Russian agreement about the border at his talks in Paris in April 1965; *Die Welt*, 3 May 1965.

[29] *Frankfurter Allgemeine Zeitung*, 2 and 4 Jan. 1965; see also Senator John Fulbright's speech before the Society on Foreign Affairs, Vienna, in May 1965, *Osterreichische Zeitschrift für Aussenpolitik*, iv/5 (1965).

territorial integrity of all European states', as a common goal of both countries.) A British government spokesman explained Brown's remarks by stating that Britain still regarded the frontier as a matter to be settled at a peace conference, but that she wanted to see the wishes of the Polish inhabitants of the former German territories taken into account.[30]

The change of attitude in the West coincided with an evolution of opinion and policy taking place in West Germany herself. To be sure, the official legal position on the Oder–Neisse line is unchanged to this day, namely that Germany's eastern frontier can only be finally determined at a peace conference, but it had begun to be challenged by public opinion. An attack by the philosopher Karl Jaspers on the whole fabric of West German policy on the East, including Poland, initiated wide discussion.[31] Considerable and protracted controversy was caused by two Protestant contributions: a memorandum of eight prominent Protestant personalities in 1962,[32] and in particular the memorandum of the Evangelical Church in Germany of October 1965,[33] both of which criticized West German policy on the Oder–Neisse Line. The impact of the Church's memorandum cannot be overemphasized. Notably its attack on the German 'right to the homeland' introduced a new element in the public debate: in the areas taken over by Poland after 1945, the 'right to the homeland' would extend to about half of the Polish population, since it was born there. Consequently the claims of these Poles (whose number was steadily growing) would clash with the claims of the refugee Germans (whose number was steadily decreasing and who had been successfully integrated in West German society). The initial public debate on the Oder–Neisse line gave further momentum to the discussion on the larger problem of Bonn's *Deutschlandpolitik* which had started earlier; many of the main contributions, which we shall examine further below, contained critical references to West Germany's border policy.

[30] See *New York Times*, 15 Feb. 1967.

[31] See Karl Jaspers, *Lebensfragen der deutschen Politik* (1963), pp. 171–249.

[32] *Süddeutsche Zeitung*, 26 Feb. 1962.

[33] For text and discussion see Reinhard Henkys, ed., *Deutschland und die östlichen Nachbarn* (1966) and Ludwig Raiser, 'Deutsche Ostpolitik im Lichte der Denkschrift der evangelischen Kirche', *Europa-Archiv*, Mar. 1966, pp. 195–208.

In the mid-1960s official spokesmen, too, began to couch the problem in terms that would have been unthinkable a few years earlier. No less a personage than the then Foreign Minister Schröder said: 'The expulsion of millions of Germans from their homeland was a blatant injustice. But we do not want to take revenge by inflicting new injustice.'[34] From the opposition, the then Vice-Chairman of the SPD, Fritz Erler, suggested the initiation of preliminary talks with the Poles about the future frontiers of a reunited Germany. During the elections of 1965 all parties carefully avoided deviating from the orthodox position. In fact, they restated it vigorously when at the height of the electoral campaign the Polish Premier, then on a visit to Paris, reiterated Poland's policy of regarding the Oder–Neisse line as the final German–Polish frontier.[35] But after the elections the controversies provoked by the memorandum of the Evangelical Church affected both major parties. Within the SPD, the left wing of the Berlin party attacked the official party line on the eastern frontiers as well as the activities of the refugee organizations, then headed by a Social Democrat, the late Wenzel Jaksch, whereas Jaksch himself vigorously protested against the memorandum.[36] Within the CDU, the chairman of a *Land* party resigned in protest over government policy on the frontiers and supported the proposals of the Evangelical Church.[37]

In a major attempt to mend fences with Eastern Europe, the so-called 'Peace Note' of March 1966 offered to transform the previously unilateral West German renunciation of the use of force in international disputes into mutual agreements with the East European governments,[38] although some of its formulations and its reference to the German borders of 1937 had the contrary effect. This may have been one reason why this effort did not immediately improve German–East European rela-

[34] *Bulletin*, 7 Apr. 1964.

[35] For his views and the German reaction see *Le Monde*, 12–13 and 16 Sept. 1965; *Europa-Archiv*, Oct. 1965.

[36] *Die Zeit*, 12 Oct. 1965 (the dates given for *Die Zeit* are always those of the North American edition); *Die Welt*, 23 Oct. 1965.

[37] *New York Times*, 9 Nov. 1965.

[38] The note made a number of other proposals that cannot be dealt with here. For the text and a number of replies from other countries see *Europa-Archiv*, Apr. and June 1966.

tions. Nevertheless it heralded a new phase in official West German thinking, which suggests potential for further evolution in West German policy. During 1966 voices from the two major parties indicated that contrary to earlier practice the questions of frontier revision and of reunification were being treated as connected issues. Within the CDU, Federal Minister Gradl suggested that 'the renunciation of a piece of East German territory [meaning beyond the Oder–Neisse line] would be a reasonable price to pay for reunification, since no one could expect it to take place within the 1937 boundaries.[39] Within the opposition, in turn, disagreement with the old policies was more outspoken. As Schmidt put it:

An unrestricted claim to our former eastern borders would give Eastern Europe in general and Poland in particular an insurmountable reason to reject not only reunification but also a normalization of relations with the Federal Republic . . . [We must leave] no doubt about our own realization that, even under most favourable circumstances, eventual reunification requires sacrifices with regard to the borders of a reunited country.[40]

During the first fifteen years of the Federal Republic the two issues had usually been treated as separate problems, and as a result the potentialities of a territorial agreement as a means to foster progress on reunification were not examined, let alone exploited. But, as Brzezinski has observed, the East Europeans have always treated the two issues as different aspects of the same German problem. Therefore, Germany was pursuing what were mutually incompatible goals: reunification and frontier revision; 'the very linkage of the two tended to reinforce the East European stake in keeping Germany divided'.[41]

West Germany's political élites, then, evidently perceive new opportunities for a *Deutschlandpolitik* in two related ways: a direct link connecting German border concessions in a *quid pro quo* with eastern measures towards overcoming or alleviating the division; and, second, an indirect strategy treating German

[39] *Der Spiegel*, 17 Jan. 1966.
[40] See p. 17 n. 9.
[41] Zbigniew Brzezinski, *Alternative to Partition; For a Broader Conception of America's Role in Europe* (1965), p. 91.

recognition of the Oder–Neisse line as a major contribution to the relaxation of tensions in Europe and hence to an ultimate solution of the German problem.

The formation of the Great Coalition introduced further elements of compromise into the West German attitude. The new government changed its terminology, removing from official vocabulary the term 'Middle Germany' for East Germany, a phrase regarded as particularly offensive by the Poles, to whom it implied that Germany claimed her own territory east of the Oder–Neisse. But, equally important, the usual reference in official pronouncements to the borders of 1937 disappeared, and the tone of statements on the border issue changed considerably.[42] The terms used by Chancellor Kiesinger on West Germany's relations with Poland are an example of the new approach:

All strata of German society share the deep desire for a reconciliation with Poland, whose painful history we have not forgotten and whose longing to live at last in a unified state territory with secure borders we understand better than ever before, in view of the present situation of our own divided people. But the borders of a reunited Germany can only be fixed by an all-German government in a settlement freely arrived at, a settlement that must create the conditions for a lasting and peaceful relationship of good neighbourliness approved by both peoples.[43]

On the issue of the Sudeten part of Czechoslovakia and the Munich Agreement of 1938, the change in West German attitudes went significantly further. For reasons alluded to above, the Czech government was anxious to have the Federal Republic, as the successor to the Third Reich, declare the Munich Agreement invalid *ex tunc*, i.e. from the very beginning as if it had never been concluded. But the German government refused to take this step. Political pressure from the refugees was as important in this refusal as the consideration that it would turn the expellees into Czech citizens. In 1964, however, Chancellor Erhard declared that the Munich Agree-

---

[42] See the Government Declaration of 13 Dec. 1966, *Bulletin*, 14 Dec. 1966, and the text of a speech by Chancellor Kiesinger at Oberhausen of 11 Feb. 1967, *Bulletin*, 15 Feb. 1967.

[43] Speech delivered at Oberhausen, *Bulletin*, 15 Feb. 1967.

ment 'was torn to pieces by Hitler' and that Germany 'has no territorial claim whatsoever with regard to Czechoslovakia and separates itself expressly from any declarations which have given rise to a different interpretation'.[44] Again, the Great Coalition government tried to bring the matter to a close. In the government declaration of December 1966, Chancellor Kiesinger, in unprecedentedly friendly and compromising tones, declared that the Munich Agreement was 'no longer valid', though he stopped short of an invalidation *ex tunc*. He also suggested settling the nationality problem and other questions in bilateral negotiations.

Such negotiations began soon thereafter, but only after protracted deliberations did Prague and Bonn reach an agreement in August 1967 to establish trade missions and to renew with some revisions their previous commercial treaty.[45] The opening of diplomatic relations which the Federal Republic had sought and hoped for did not come about. Of course, the exact reasons will not become public knowledge for some time, but it became known that Prague had put forward demands which the German negotiators could not accept. Czechoslovakia had been under heavy pressure from Russia and East Germany, both of which were eager to stall the Great Coalition's diplomatic offensive in Eastern Europe. East Berlin had asked all its socialist allies to make diplomatic relations with Bonn dependent upon prior West German recognition of the GDR, the existing frontiers, and a complete renunciation of any nuclear role—issues which were apparently raised by the Czech negotiators.[46] Prague insisted on its previous demand

[44] Speech before the Council on Foreign Relations on 11 June 1964, *Bulletin*, 12 June 1964.

[45] *Süddeutsche Zeitung*, 4 Aug. 1967.

[46] These three demands had been laid down in the Bucharest declaration of July 1966 of the Warsaw Pact countries, but not in connexion with diplomatic relations with Bonn (for the text see *Europa-Archiv*, Aug. 1966). An attempt to commit the Warsaw Pact governments to make West German acceptance of these demands a condition for their diplomatic relations with Bonn, made at the Warsaw meeting in February 1967, failed, apparently because of Rumanian objections (see the *New York Times*, 11 Feb. 1967). The Treaty of Friendship, Co-operation, and Mutual Assistance which the East Germans concluded with Prague in March 1967 as part of their counter-offensive to the Federal Republic's initiatives in Eastern Europe, mentioned the necessity for West German recognition of the GDR and the frontiers, but, again, not in connexion with diplomatic relations with Bonn (for the text see *Europa-Archiv*, Apr. 1967). These facts show

that the Federal Republic go all the way to an invalidation of the Munich Agreement *ex tunc*. But, given Czechoslovakia's previous policy, which gave unequivocal priority to a settlement of the Sudeten issue, the decisive factor in preventing the establishment of diplomatic relations was most probably pressure on Prague by the Soviet Union and East Germany. However, Bonn seems to accept the viewpoint of many of its domestic critics that sticking to a last legal point is not worth the price of having no relations with Czechoslovakia. In an *aide-memoire* to the Soviet Union of 9 April 1968, on the renunciation of the use of force, Bonn was reported to have offered negotiations about an *ex tunc* invalidation. The case could conceivably be opened again, once the Czech leaders have gained more leeway for such action within their own camp.

Problems of a solution

Thus, while the Western powers have reason to hope that the Sudeten issue can and will be settled, the Oder–Neisse problem is still prominent as one of the potentially disruptive problems of Europe. Public opinion and political élites in West Germany have given increasing support to a settlement. They were strengthened considerably when in 1968 a Catholic lay organization followed the precedent of the Protestant Church and supported a qualified recognition of the frontier.[47] Nevertheless, a majority of the responsible élites still reject any recognition of the Oder–Neisse line on the grounds that it would be tantamount to throwing away the claim to one-quarter of Germany's former territory, held for many centuries, while getting nothing in return.

Many sectors of public opinion in the West would agree with the argument of certain West German critics that this position, far from preserving a bargaining asset from whose release immediate returns can be expected, actually jeopardizes West

that despite heavy pressure, Czechoslovakia like other Socialist countries succeeded in preserving a small amount of freedom of manoeuvre for future action *vis-à-vis* West Germany.

[47] Bensberger Kreis, *Ein Memorandum Deutscher Katholiken zu den polnisch-deutschen Fragen* (1968).

Germany's interests by playing into the hands of those Communist leaders who are not interested in friendlier relations with West Germany. As long as the Federal Republic maintains territorial claims on other countries, it is fairly easy for the Communists to depict her as *revanchist* and a menace to peace in Europe. Even progressive 'peace notes' and solemn renunciations of force will lack credibility to them. Moreover, time and history work against the Federal Republic; by now the belief that the lost German territories can be regained peacefully is perhaps illusory; some years hence it will be an anachronism, and a dangerous one, too.

Domestic critics of official German policy have often been motivated by a desire to reactivate intra-German policies and improve conditions with a view to alleviating the division. And, indeed, it could be argued that if a German recognition of the Oder–Neisse line has any political potential at all—and this postulate loses value with every passing year—it is in relation to a policy of either using German border concessions as a *quid pro quo* for Communist moves to alleviate the division, or treating recognition of the present border as a German contribution to the relaxation of tensions in Europe and thereby improving the long-term conditions for progress on the unification issue.

If, to repeat a suggestion made in 1965,[48] the Federal Republic were to recognize the Oder–Neisse line as the definitive frontier of a *reunited* Germany, and if this recognition were accompanied by firm Western guarantees, she might be able to establish the link between reunification and the border issue that would generate some real interest in German unity, at least in Poland. This step could be a 'conditional recognition' to take effect only *after* progress on German reunification had reached a stage previously defined in negotiations. This formula has the advantage of offering a flexible framework for all parties involved, into which practically any definition of 'reunification' will fit. Equally important, it would partially disarm a nationalist right in West Germany, which threatens to attack the government for making unilateral concessions, for it postpones effective concessions into the future while simultaneously

[48] Kaiser, *Frankfurter Hefte*, Nov. 1965.

creating concrete returns. A 'conditional recognition' would enable the West German government to place the stigma of un-patriotic behaviour on the opponents of this step.

This approach is supported by survey data. The results differ greatly according to the formulation of the question. Asked whether they would 'recognize' the Oder–Neisse line, 19% of the interviewees of an EMNID poll gave affirmative and 51% negative answers (June 1967); asked whether the Germans should 'resign' themselves to the new frontier, a survey of the Allensbach Institute found out that 35% were for and 43% against it (October 1967). But when asked whether the Oder–Neisse line should be 'recognized if, in return, unity were achieved', 50% were for and 25% against (Allensbach, 1966); the ratio was 53% for and 33% against 'if recognition were to produce better relations with the East' (Allensbach, 7 Nov. 1967).

Among the West German parties, the FDP came nearest to such a position at its 1967 party conference. After bitter debates which occasionally threatened to break the unity of the party, the congress narrowly rejected the demand of an outspoken group to endorse recognition of the Oder–Neisse line and, instead, stipulated in its call for a new *Deutschlandpolitik* 'that a possible rapprochement of the separate parts of Germany should not founder on territorial questions'.[49]

It may be indicative of the potential impact of a border agreement on intra-German relations that the East German leaders seem to be afraid of it. They are aware that West German concessions on the borders could create a Polish–West German understanding that could possibly threaten their position. Ulbricht himself declared in May 1965 that the Federal Republic, with the full backing of the United States, had made it understood in socialist countries that, except for 'small, purely formal border corrections', she would recognize the present Oder–Neisse line if the socialist governments were to support a reunification of Germany. He went on to denounce such a proposition as an 'old imperialist gimmick to deceive the other [socialist] states in order to divide them, put them under pres-

---

[49] See *Die Zeit*, 21 and 28 Mar. 1967; *Süddeutsche Zeitung*, 5 and 6 Apr. 1967; *Die Welt*, 7 Apr. 1967.

sure, blackmail them, and, if possible, defeat them separately'.[50]

Not surprisingly, the legal, political, and strategic arguments against recognition of the Oder–Neisse line within Germany have deep emotional roots whose strength may account for the contradictions between different components of West Germany's policy towards the East. One contradiction attracts particular attention because it is contained in an argument repeated almost *ad nauseam* in Germany: how can the Poles recognize East Germany as a state, it is asked, and also expect the West Germans to recognize the border of what is then another state? The Federal Republic can only recognize her own borders; any other German frontier can be fixed or recognized only by the government of a united Germany.[51] This argument contradicts a central tenet of West German foreign policy: that the Federal Republic represents the only freely constituted German government that can speak in the name of all Germans. According to the logic of this claim, she is entitled to make a decision on Germany's eastern frontiers on behalf of all Germans. Moreover, it can be argued that the recognition of frontiers by states not adjacent to them has always been a major foreign-policy instrument and was for centuries the subject of international agreements. Certainly Germany would be entitled to use this instrument—whatever the exact nature of such an agreement—since this issue is of direct and crucial importance to her political future.

While growing flexibility on the border issue among West Germany's political leaders seems to improve the prospects for a solution in one sense, in another sense settlement has been rendered more difficult because of the stiffening Polish attitude. In the early 1950s Poland was still eager to open diplomatic relations with the Federal Republic unconditionally. Now she is unwilling to do so without West German recognition of both the Oder–Neisse line *and* the GDR (as well as complete West German abstinence from any nuclear role).

It could be argued that Poland desires more freedom from Moscow but cannot achieve it so long as the territorial dispute with Germany is unsettled, since this constitutes the main

[50] *Neues Deutschland*, 6 May 1965.
[51] e.g., Rainer Barzel, *Gesichtspunkte eines Deutschen* (1968), p. 233.

source of Polish fear of the Federal Republic. According to this argument, it is most unlikely that the Polish government would reject a reasonable West German offer and the opportunity to gain final Western acceptance and guarantee of Poland's western borders. This would give her more freedom of manoeuvre *vis-à-vis* the Soviet Union at the price of supporting progress towards a reunified Germany which she would no longer have cause to fear.

Sceptics reply that the Poles have no interest in German unity, Communist or capitalist, and that the present Polish leaders want to maintain the border dispute in order to enlist the support of a wary population. According to this school of thought, West German recognition of the frontier might even embarrass them by depriving them of some of the arguments previously used against Bonn: recognition might well be simply cast aside as not being credible and denounced as evidence of a different kind of German *revanchism* which has learned to disguise itself more skilfully. Some evidence for this point was provided by the unusually bitter attacks which the Polish government made on the Polish episcopate after the bishops had sent a letter to their German counterparts on the occasion of the Vatican Council in November 1965, in which they addressed themselves to the Oder–Neisse problem in a relatively conciliatory manner (though on the other hand, this incident has to be placed in the context of the Church–State struggle in Poland).[52]

Not surprisingly, the present West German government is reluctant to make what it regards as a major concession without some certainty that it will have the desired effect on the Polish leaders. It is at this point that Western diplomacy faces the difficult task of reconciling two kinds of intransigence. For these reasons their problem is by no means simply how to put pressure on a reluctant German government, as is often suggested. Involvement, mediation, and persuasion in Eastern Europe is also necessary to break the vicious circle of the past.

Finally, it is doubtful whether German recognition of the Oder–Neisse line alone will represent progress if it has disrup-

[52] For the texts, see Reinhard Henkys, ed., *Deutschland und die östlichen Nachbarn*, (1966) and the *New York Times*, 20 Dec. 1965.

tive consequences in other areas—including West Germany's domestic politics. While the domestic margin of manoeuvre available to West German leaders is larger than it was a few years ago, it may still be too narrow for radical measures.

West German territorial concessions made as a result of clumsily applied Western pressure may well mortgage the future. As a lucid observer of German politics, Karl-Dietrich Bracher, has rightly pointed out, the extreme right in West Germany, which since 1966 has experienced a small but significant revival, already approaches the question in terms reminiscent of those used during the Weimar Republic, accusing the present leaders of *Erfüllungspolitik* (policy of fulfilment) in too easily accepting the *Diktat* of the World War II victors.[53] Needless to say, West Germany's political leaders are aware of this threat. They have constantly used it as an argument against advocates of frontier recognition in order to justify their own more cautious policy.[54]

On the other hand, as German critics of past Bonn policies have often pointed out, governments are not pawns in the hands of their public but can influence public opinion through courageous and convincing leadership. To do so requires, however, that a majority of those in key positions are convinced of the wisdom of the move, which is not the case in the Federal Republic. The Great Coalition offers a unique and historical opportunity to make a courageous, albeit in the short run, unpopular, decision. United, the two major parties may be able to contain the (probably temporary) appeal of an extreme right trying to capture the discontented vote; opposing each other, they could not even move on the border issue for fear of losing the marginal vote they need to come to or stay in power.

During its 1968 party conference the SPD moved another

[53] Karl-Dietrich Bracher, 'Wird Bonn doch Weimar?', *Der Spiegel*, 13 Mar. 1967.

[54] Chancellor Kiesinger was quoted in *Der Stern* (23 Oct. 1967) as having said: 'This [the recognition of the Oder–Neisse line] no doubt would greatly facilitate our foreign policy in both East and West but it could generate a wave of right-wing radicalism in the Federal Republic. I do not want to expose ourselves to this danger.' This statement not only reflected the views of many German politicians, but the fact that it had to be denied afterwards because of a wave of criticism shows how strong opposition to a change in frontier policy still is.

step away from the orthodox position by declaring that an improvement of relations with Eastern Europe would be made easier if the Federal Republic would 'respect and recognize the existing borders in Europe, particularly the present western frontier of Poland, until the German borders are definitely delineated in a peace settlement recognized by all parties involved as just and permanent'.[55] However, the CDU coalition partner rejected this position which amounted to a *de facto* recognition of the border until a final settlement. In fact, Chancellor Kiesinger regretted this choice of words which could be 'misused at home and abroad' and restated the previous policy of the German government.[56]

[55] *Die Welt*, 21 Mar. 1968.
[56] The *New York Times*, 28 Mar. 1968.

5

PRIORITIES FOR THE WEST:
IS REUNIFICATION STILL THE ISSUE?

AMONG the paradoxes of the present international system in the northern hemisphere, one is particularly relevant to the German problem. A policy of movement between East and West has become possible because the major actors, including the two German régimes, have accepted the overall structure of a divided Europe while explicitly professing that the policy of movement aims at overcoming it.

East and West now share the conviction that ceasing to threaten the other's survival is the precondition for peaceful change, and both aim towards change through gradual accommodation and mutual involvement within the superstructure of 'muted bipolarity'. For all practical purposes both German régimes now accept the division of the German nation—in order to overcome it. It is a characteristic feature of present-day Europe that accommodation to the *status quo* sets free forces that inherently challenge it.

This paradox raises a host of questions about the division of Germany. If radical change of the international system is impossible and too dangerous, will the partition of Germany continue for a long period of time, since it is here that change can most easily upset stability? Put differently, to what extent does a 'policy of movement' in Europe *presuppose* Germany's partition? Is the reunification of two powerful industrial states in the centre of Europe into one unit of seventy-seven million Germans a feasible solution and does it make sense to support it as a goal of Western policy?

The problem does not end here. Can a rapprochement and better understanding between Western and Communist countries have a genuine and lasting effect in Europe, if it bypasses the centre of the continent and leaves Germany divided? This raises the intriguing question whether there are solutions other than the reconstitution of a united German state that could muster the support of both Germans and non-Germans. It becomes increasingly unclear what is generally meant when one refers to reunification as a solution to the German problem. Nor is it clear whether Western policy can afford to abandon support for the objective of ultimate German unity.

Obstacles and opposition to reunification

Within the West, each country views the German problem and possible future solutions according to its particular national situation and interests, but there are certain common themes which deserve closer examination.

Opposition to the restoration of a united German state normally derives from three basic concerns: first, apprehension that the mere attempt to move towards unification—even the first step—might be enough to destabilize the situation in Europe; second, fear of the sheer might of a reunited Germany; and, third, concern that reunification would result in the ultimate destabilization of Europe anyway because the safeguards may last only temporarily.

It is true that a divided Germany has become part of the existing, though precarious, balance of power in Europe, notwithstanding the human suffering it entails in the form of suppression of democratic liberties in the East, separation of families, and killings at the intra-German frontiers. Each side is opposed to reunification on the terms of the other, and each can effectively prevent it. As the late President Kennedy put it in November 1961, 'there are going to be two Germanies as long as the Soviet Union believes that that is in her interest'[57]—and, one could add, as long as the United States cannot accept a reunited Communist Germany.

The fact that a mere attempt to come to terms with this complex issue might upset the European equilibrium was one reason why Adenauer, with the support of American diplomacy, refused even to consider Soviet offers concerning it—such as those in the famous note of 1952—or opposition proposals for neutralization. And it is for this reason that concrete Western proposals for overcoming Europe's division—even de Gaulle's, as we shall see—generally bypass the German issue for an initial

[57] In an interview with Aleksey Adzhubey (editor of *Izvestia*), *New York Times*, 29 Nov. 1961.

period of time. There is a widespread desire among Western governments not to rouse sleeping dogs and to bypass this explosive and intractable problem in their efforts to achieve *détente*. This tendency frequently gives Western calls for initiatives towards reunification or endorsements of unity a rhetorical character.

There is not only opposition to reunification on Communist terms. The possibility of merging the two German states on Western terms often causes misgivings, if not outright opposition. The Federal Republic has become one of the world's principal economic powers. To be sure, this has not been accompanied by a parallel increase in political influence, partly because she has not chosen to use her economic weight for international political ends. But her standing in the world community has risen steadily, and, no doubt, her economic resources have contributed to this development. In a world where nation-states increasingly act without some of the restraints imposed on them by conditions of the immediate postwar years, her economic success is viewed not without concern by those who remember what German foreign policy, pursued from a position of strength, has been like. There is naturally, then, a certain apprehension about a merger of the two parts of Germany, since this would create an economic power of the first magnitude.

West Germany alone is a country with formidable resources. Not only is she the most populous state of Western Europe, but her highly skilled population, equipped with sophisticated technology and managerial capabilities, has made her the foremost economic power in Europe, next to the Soviet Union, and the world's second leading exporter. Her GNP is Western Europe's highest, and her armed forces are generally regarded as the strongest conventional ones among European members of NATO.

Just as West Germany is the second industrial power in the West, so East Germany is the second industrial power in the East—a point not always acknowledged. Political propaganda, the Federal Republic's relatively successful policy of isolating her, a number of obvious economic failures, and the régime's political difficulties have considerably blurred the reality of

East Germany in the eyes of the world. Though her population is only about one-third of that of the Federal Republic, the GDR ranks among the ten leading industrial states of the world. Within the COMECON countries, East Germany's exports in 1966 were exceeded only by those of the Soviet Union, and her standard of living is generally regarded as the highest in the Communist world. It is therefore not without reason that the régime is proud of its achievements. In 1965 her leaders could declare that the Soviet Union no longer served as a model in all areas of economic management; in fact, the Soviet Union was now learning from the application of the 'new economic system' in the GDR.[58]

East Germany's economic performance is all the more remarkable if one considers the handicaps to her recovery. While her Western neighbour reconstructed the country with some $10 billion of aid received from 1947 onwards, East Germany had to pay approximately the same amount in reparations to the Soviet Union until the mid-1950s.[59] A politically oriented and sometimes disastrous economic policy, as well as heavy manpower losses as refugees fled to the West, impeded the rational utilization of existing resources. Moreover, the amputation of the Reich's economically complementary territories in the east and the west was far more detrimental to East Germany than to the Federal Republic.

What entity would emerge from a unification of the two parts of Germany? The comparisons made in the table on p. 54 outline the new unit's order of magnitude. These few figures suggest a conclusion that can easily be substantiated by more evidence: the reunification of the two Germanies would create a dynamic economic power of formidable resources in the heart of Europe. Such a prospect, often all too easily judged against the past, does cause some negative reactions in other nations. As a French journalist of left-wing sympathies put it (his perhaps overdramatic expression reflects the European left's particular

[58] See the address of Peter Florin, member of the Central Committee of the SED, to the Society for German-Soviet Friendship, published as a special supplement of *Presse der Sowjetunion*, no. 64 (1965).

[59] For details, see Karl W. Deutsch and Lewis J. Edinger, *Germany Rejoins the Powers* (1959), pp. 145–53; Ernst Richert, *Das Zweite Deutschland*, (1964) pp. 242–5.

C

Comparative Economic Standing of a Reunited Germany

Population (in mn, mid-year 1967)		Total Exports (in bn of US $, 1967)	
USSR	235·6	US	31·2
USA	199·1	*Reunited Germany*	25·0
Japan	99·9	West Germany	21·7
Reunited Germany	77·0	UK	13·4
West Germany	59·9	France	11·4
UK	55·1	Japan	10·4
Italy	52·3	Italy	8·7
France	49·9	USSR	8·7*
Poland	31·9	East Germany	3·3*
East Germany	17·1	Czechoslovakia (1966)	2·7
Czechoslovakia	14·3	Poland (1966)	2·3

* Estimated from 1965 figures.

Crude Steel Production (in mn metric tons, 1966)		Gross National Product (in bn of US $, 1966)	
USA	121·5	US	759·3
USSR	96·8	USSR	322·5*
Japan	43·1	*Reunited Germany*	146·7
Reunited Germany	39·1	West Germany	120·2
West Germany	35·0	UK	96·3
UK	24.7	France	93·2
France	19·6	Japan	83·9
Italy	13·6	Italy	56·5
Poland	9·9	Poland	26·5†
Czechoslovakia	9·1	East Germany	23·1†
East Germany	4·1	Czechoslovakia	19·4†

* Estimated from 1964 figures and projected 1960–5 average growth rates (*source:* Cohn, 'Soviet Growth Retardation', below).

† Estimated from 1964 figures and projected 1951–64 average growth rates (*source:* Ernst, 'Postwar Economic Growth', below).

Sources: UN *Monthly B. Statist.*, Jan & May 1967 & May 1968; IMF, *International Financial Statistics*, June 1967, GNP calculated on basis of official exchange rates; Stanley H. Cohn, 'Soviet Growth Retardation: Trends in Resource Availability and Efficiency', in US Congress, Joint Economic Cttee, 89th Congress, 2nd sess., Washington, 1966, *New Directions in the Soviet Economy*, pt. iiA, pp. 109, 127; Maurice Ernst, 'Postwar Economic Growth in Eastern Europe' (A Comparison with Western Europe), ibid. pt. iv, pp. 877, 880.

reservations): 'Such a Germany, even if neutral, would be a country whose economic weight would make Europe tremble.'[60] Thus, the old structural problem of Europe, namely of how to accommodate in the European state system a country of eighty million inhabitants which is larger than all the others except Russia, reappears in the contemporary resistance to a merger of the two German states.

To most nations with a stake in Europe, however, the main importance of reunification lies not merely in the combination of East and West German economic capabilities, important though this is. The prime significance may—more correctly— be seen in the removal of those restrictions on both parts of Germany which at present arise from her division. To be sure, these parallel restrictions resulted from Germany's defeat in 1945, but as this event recedes into history it gradually de- creases in importance as a rationale for limiting German sovereignty. A second rationale remains effective, however, the importance of which cannot be overemphasized. The Federal Republic accepted and continues to accept the position of a junior partner in the West and a secondary power in Western Europe as a West German contribution to and in order to muster her allies' indispensable support for German reunifica- tion. Even if the Federal Republic were to reject past policy and claim an autonomous role in international politics, her free- dom of diplomatic manoeuvre would still be sharply limited, and she would be unable to use all her capabilities—that is as long as Germany remained divided and Berlin exposed, on the one hand, and she adhered to German unity and the freedom of the former capital as vital policy objectives, on the other. Similar considerations apply to East Germany, which must painstakingly follow the course set by Moscow in foreign and military policies.

A reunified Germany would not, therefore, simply be the sum of two existing states. She would occupy an entirely new category—that of a nation whose power fell short of that of the two super-powers but considerably ahead (except for the possession of nuclear weapons) of Europe's traditional great powers like Britain and France. Moreover, reunification would

[60] Gérard Sandoz, *Le Nouvel Observateur*, 6 May 1965.

liberate additional forces, since East and West Germany now use up much energy in challenging each other.

These considerations may seem only theoretical, since they postulate German unity while neglecting the very conditions on which unification would depend. Indeed, it is hardly conceivable that reunification will occur without a fundamental change of the international system, one that reconciled German unity with the basic interests of the nations that have a say in bringing it about. This probably means prior agreements on arms control, on alliance structure, or European integration that set forth restrictions upon, and an acceptable role for, a united Germany. And, in fact, few forces in East or West believe that German reunification is possible without stringent and effective safeguards making it internationally acceptable. But would these safeguards be effective in the long run and guarantee stability in the Europe of the future? History, especially European history, abounds with examples of international agreements and national restrictions being broken—often with tragic consequences. Germany herself between the two world wars provided examples that her European neighbours have not forgotten. Moreover, of the possible restrictions on a unified Germany, neutralization, which comes most quickly to mind, seems to many Europeans fraught with risks. The unit to be neutralized would not, after all, be an Austria or Switzerland, but the second industrial power of Europe.

In short, even the initiation of serious moves towards German unity is frequently believed to conflict with the national interests of European countries. This view is corroborated by the historical images against which German unity is measured—images which are no less powerful for being possibly outmoded. At the same time, the contemplation of alternative frameworks for an acceptable German unity is an even harder exercise, in which uncertainty inevitably prevails.

Any discussion of obstacles and opposition to reunification would be incomplete without mention of the policy of the Soviet Union, since she has a major interest in Germany and exercises a major influence on all matters related to the German problem. Only a few aspects, important to our discussion, will be examined here, since the main emphasis of this essay lies on the implications of the German problem for the West.

A digression: Soviet policy on Germany's division

Soviet policy towards Germany after World War II has been characterized by the double ambiguity of a 'close relationship between expansionist aspirations and consolidationist tendencies' on the one hand, and the uncertainty whether to pursue her own interests within the framework of a united or divided Germany on the other.[61] Soviet interest in a *détente* notwithstanding, the first ambiguity remains relevant today; the second may appear less so under present circumstances, since for the time being the Russians seem to regard a divided Germany as the most useful for their interests; but the increasing flexibility and variety of Western policies offer new opportunities for an active Soviet diplomacy on the German problem in which the old ambiguity might be reasserted. It is by no means to be excluded that the Soviet Union may try again to play the card of German unity, by offering to accept it in the context of a changed system of alliances, in particular with Germany neutralized.

For the Soviet Union, any kind of German reunification on other than her own terms raises many interconnected issues concerning her own security, her future relations with the West in general and Western Europe in particular, her already weakening control over Eastern Europe, the future course of 'world revolution', and, finally, but not least important, her position in the Communist world movement. A unified Germany, whether Western or neutral, to the Russians means above all the loss of East Germany, with possibly detrimental consequences in most of the crucial areas mentioned. The danger of 'losing' the GDR is obvious in the case of reunification on past Western terms, but Soviet leaders have viewed even a neutralized Germany in a similar way. As Khrushchev

---

[61] Melvin Croan, 'Eastern Policy and the Dilemmas of Germany's Division', unpubl. paper for the Center for International Affairs, Harvard University, Dec. 1965. See also his 'Reality and Illusion in Soviet-German Relations', *Survey*, Oct. 1962, pp. 12–28.

put it to Guy Mollet in 1956, 'I prefer having 20 million Germans on my side to having 70 million against us. Even if Germany were militarily neutral, it would not be sufficient for us.'[62]

What would be the consequences of East Germany leaving the Soviet orbit? Militarily, the loss of her armed forces and territory would change the balance between NATO and the Warsaw Pact, since East Germany serves as a military buffer zone for Poland and protects Czechoslovakia's flank. Soviet and East German military spokesmen gave emphasis to this, for example, in the *Oktobersturm* manoeuvres which the Warsaw Pact countries organized on GDR soil in 1965. Judging by the propaganda campaign that the Socialist Unity Party (SED) launched on this occasion, the main purpose of these exercises seemed to have been to demonstrate to Soviet military leaders, and thus indirectly to Soviet political leaders, that the GDR's contribution had become indispensable to the defence of Soviet interests, especially as a counterweight to the steadily growing power of the Federal Republic.

From an economic point of view a severing of links between the GDR and the socialist states would separate the second most important industrial power from the system of specialization that has developed among the COMECON countries. In recent years the GDR has been exporting an average of one industrial plant a week, and has supplied much of the capital equipment for her COMECON associates. Among all members of this grouping, the COMECON share in her foreign trade is the highest, the Western share (excluding the Federal Republic's) the lowest. She is therefore an indispensable partner.[63] Since this economic interdependence and co-operation among the socialist states is a supporting element of great importance to the Soviet Union's political influence, the change to a united Germany would considerably jeopardize that influence within the socialist camp. Moreover, the East German contribution to the Soviet economy is important: one-fifth of Russian im-

[62] *Bulletin*, 20 July 1956.

[63] On these problems, see Hans-Dieter Schulz, 'Moskaus wichtigster Partner: Die Stellung der "DDR" im Ostblock', *Europa-Archiv*, Nov. 1964, pp. 785–94; and Kurt P. Tudyka, 'Die DDR im Kräftefeld des Ost-West Konflikts', *Europa-Archiv*, Jan. 1966, pp. 16–27.

ports, primarily highly specialized capital equipment, originate in the GDR, and East Germany is a major recipient of Soviet raw materials.

Naturally, the conditions under which German reunification came about would determine whether and to what extent the GDR's present economic links with Eastern Europe would be preserved. At this stage, however, the point is of only theoretical importance; rightly or wrongly, the socialist countries tend to believe that a merger of East Germany with the more powerful capitalist economy of West Germany would mean the economic loss of the GDR for the socialist camp. They have an economic stake in the present system of co-operation with East Germany, and any realistic assessment of the German problem and possible solutions will have to take account of these interests.

If East Germany, the Soviet Union's outpost and most important ally in the heart of Europe, joined a westernized or neutralized Germany, she would remove the most important barrier between the West and the socialist states, and would no doubt tremendously undermine the prestige of the Soviet Union. This would give further momentum to the trend among East European countries to achieve greater independence from Moscow. In fact, it might possibly deliver a fatal blow to the present international system of socialist states, and the dominant role of the Soviet Union in it, in Eastern Europe. In particular, Czechoslovakia, a country with strong cultural and historical links with the West, might move closer to Western Europe.

As long as there is a close identification of vital interests in security, ideology, and trade between East European leaders and the 'first socialist state on German soil', the former will have an interest in preserving the German division. In fact, the intra-German antagonism offers them opportunities to wrest economic concessions from East Germany as a premium for maintaining loyalty towards a socialist ally in their dealings with the Federal Republic (somewhat similar to the concessions extracted by neutral countries from West Germany in exchange for not recognizing the GDR). Paradoxically, the Federal Republic's activated *Ostpolitik* increases their leverage *vis-à-vis* the GDR. Hence, in the absence of a settlement of existing territorial disputes and of a clear alternative to the present economic advantage, an interest in German unity will hardly arise in these countries. This also means, however, that —at least theoretically—the Soviet Union can threaten to support German reunification in order to enforce subservience to her policy if her present means of influence should fail.

Probably most important, Soviet acceptance of a united westernized or neutralized Germany would be tantamount to a renunciation of traditionally expansionist Soviet foreign-policy goals in Europe. The orthodox Marxist–Leninist belief that a revolution in Germany is the decisive step on the road to victory of the world revolution has been further modified in the face of nuclear reality and Soviet interest in a *détente*. Despite Soviet activities in other continents, the present Soviet leaders have not abandoned their conviction that Germany is the key to Europe, nor, as Richard Löwenthal rightly reminds us, that Europe is the continent which, for several decades to come, will significantly affect the struggle between Washington, Moscow, and Peking.[64]

Finally, a reunited Germany and the consequent loss to the socialist camp would be a development for which the Soviet Union would have to take the blame. China would denounce steps in this direction as a further proof of Moscow's complicity with imperialism. In recent years the Chinese have condemned several Soviet moves as betrayals of East German interests. Among them were, for example, the June 1964 Treaty of Friendship between the GDR and the Soviet Union (signalling a Soviet retreat from previous announcements of intentions to conclude a peace treaty with the GDR), Moscow's withdrawal from its militant stance on Berlin in the 1958 ultimatum, and Soviet acceptance of the Western view that signature of the 1963 nuclear test-ban treaty did not necessarily imply recognition of the GDR, one of the co-signatories.[65] The Chinese warned other Communist leaders that if the Russians 'sell out the

---

[64] Richard Löwenthal, 'Der Einfluss Chinas auf die Entwicklung des Ost-West Konflikts in Europa', *Europa-Archiv*, May 1967.

[65] See, e.g., 'Oppose This Criminal Deal' and 'Another Deal in the Making', both in *Peking Review*, 11 Sept. 1964; see also ibid. 11 June 1965.

interests of the German Democratic Republic today, who can say that they will not bargain away the interests of another state tomorrow?'[66] These accusations touch on a sensitive spot, particularly among Poles and East Germans, who, under the surface of mutual allegiance, remain suspicious that their interests might be sacrificed by Moscow to a Soviet–American— or Soviet–West German—rapprochement.[66] To be sure, Peking's policy has been ambiguous, since China has also attempted to cultivate relations with West Germany, which it declared to be a member of 'the second intermediate zone', i.e. a potential ally against Washington and Moscow. China even appealed to German irredentist feelings by deploring the annexation of former German territory.[67]

To the Soviet Union the unification of the two parts of Germany into a non-Communist state, then, raises a multitude of different issues that call for different and at times conflicting policies. This may help to explain the ambiguity of Soviet policy on Germany in pursuing at once defensive and offensive goals. But other factors have to be examined as well.

We must place the consolidationist element in the Soviet position on Germany in the larger context of Russia's attempt to seek a relaxation of tensions with the West. The nuclear balance of terror and the resulting inability of the Soviet Union to achieve expansionist objectives by military means, together with domestic pressure for a reallocation of resources for civilian purposes, have been among the reasons for the interest in an accommodation with the West. The 'hot-line' agreement between Moscow and Washington, the Soviet signature to the 1963 limited Test-Ban Treaty, and Soviet–American consultation to avoid a military confrontation during the Middle East crisis in 1967 testify to Russia's desire to reach understandings in crucial areas in order to preserve stability. Friction in Germany, a weak spot in the international system, could easily jeopardize such a policy.

In fact, in pursuance of this objective, the Soviet Union

---

[66] *People's Daily*, quoted in *Frankfurter Allgemeine Zeitung*, 24 Aug. 1963.

[67] See Carola Stern, 'East Germany', in William E. Griffith, ed., *Communism in Europe* (1966), vol. ii, pp. 43–154; William E. Griffith, *Sino-Soviet Relations, 1964–5* (Cambridge, Mass., 1966).

seems to have repeatedly overruled East Germany's desire to pursue a more offensive policy towards the West on the issue of Berlin. This restraint found its most spectacular expression in the 1964 Treaty of Friendship between the two countries. To the disappointment of his allies in East Berlin, Khrushchev not only scrapped (at least temporarily) the objectives of the Berlin offensive that he had launched so dramatically in November 1958, but also restated Soviet adherence to the Potsdam Agreement which stipulated four-power control of Berlin and Western access to the former capital. Indeed, this reference to Western *and Soviet* responsibilities in Germany has been supported by other East European countries, which have been eager to gain the greater manoeuvrability made possible by decreased East–West tension. With regard to Berlin they did, in fact, endorse the Soviet line and resisted Ulbricht's requests for support of a more militant position couched in renewed demands to transform West Berlin into a 'free city'.[68]

To the Soviet Union maintenance of the *status quo* includes the preservation of East Germany's present social and economic system, as well as her ties with the USSR.

Russia naturally prefers this continuation of the *status quo* to changes made at her expense, which is probably why Foreign Minister Gromyko asserted in March 1965, that German unity could 'never' be realized, since the two German régimes had become fundamentally different. If any rapprochement was possible, he suggested, then it could be achieved only between the two states.[69] Otherwise, the socialist character of East Germany and her ties with the Soviet Union could be jeopardized. This same concern was at the root of numerous proposals for a 'confederation' (not reunification!) between the two states, proposals that were intended to force the West to accept the German division—which would be a net gain—and

[68] According to available evidence this happened at the January 1965 meeting of the Warsaw Pact countries. See the communiqué in *Pravda*, 22 Jan. 1965, and the treatment of the Berlin question in an Ulbricht interview over East German television on 24 Jan. 1965 (quoted in *Bericht über die Entwicklung in der Sowjetzone*, Jan. 1965, pp. 28–30, mimeo., published by the SPD, Bonn). Furthermore, the harassment tactics applied by the Soviet Union against West Berlin in retaliation against a meeting of the Bundestag in Berlin in April 1965, apparently fell considerably short of what the East German régime had wanted.

[69] During discussions with the British Government; *Die Welt*, 18/19 Mar. 1965.

to consolidate the division as a basis for further offensive diplomacy. In Brezhnev's words, 'The development of the GDR is becoming an increasingly important factor in securing the victory of socialism over capitalism in peaceful competition'.[70]

The defensive aspects of Soviet policy on Germany are closely related to its offensive elements. Russia's German policy was expansionist even before the collapse of Nazi Germany, since Stalin clearly intended not only to ensure that any settlement made after Germany's defeat would guarantee Soviet security but also to influence the future political development in *all* of Germany. Though it is difficult to discern the Russians' precise strategy in the aftermath of the armistice—and it is doubtful whether there was one—the behaviour of the Soviet authorities and their German henchmen, brought back from exile in Moscow, in the Soviet occupation zone indicated that Stalin tried to reach beyond the territory held by the Red Army. Though many initial Soviet measures, such as rapid Sovietization, 'were defensive in inspiration, they were also clearly expansionist in implication',[71] securing a Soviet foothold for further moves directed at the rest of Germany. Other, more explicitly expansionist actions ranged from appeals to German nationalism and attempts to capitalize on the Germans' desire for unity, to outright offensives such as the Berlin blockade, made in order to regain the initiative captured by the rapid and major American involvement in the western part of Germany beginning in 1946.

Soviet initiatives in the early and mid-1950s to thwart West Germany's integration into the West shifted the emphasis of expansionist measures to the realm of diplomacy. In a note of March 1952 the Soviet Union proposed negotiations on the unification of a Germany that was to be neutral but possessing her own armaments. This action had defensive implications in so far as it intended to prevent the addition of Germany's potential to the West but in the context of the prevailing East–West competition for German allegiance, the Soviet diplomatic proposals could not fail to constitute a major offensive bid to re-

[70] *Pravda*, 7 Oct. 1964.
[71] Croan, 'Eastern Policy and the Dilemmas of Germany's Division' (1965, mimeo).

gain the political initiative inside Germany. The Russians had every reason to expect political dividends whether their proposals were accepted or not.[72] The same argument can be applied to later Soviet challenges to Berlin between 1958 and 1962, which aimed at Germany as a whole, if not at the entire Western alliance in its then existing form, for a Russian success in Berlin would have seriously undermined the Federal Republic's links with the West.

With the exception of occasional skirmishes over Berlin and repeated barrages of more or less verbal hostility aimed at the Federal Republic, Russian policy since 1962 has been comparatively restrained. But to conclude that the Soviet Union has given up her expansionist objectives would be premature. Using more subtle and diplomatic means, the Russians are still engaged in what Brzezinski has called a 'policy of fragmentation' intended 'not to ease the division of Europe but to divide the non-Communist half'.[73] This policy attempts to transform differences among Western countries into major rifts. In order to succeed, the Soviet Union need not draw only on conflicting Western policies and ambitions; she can also create new conflicts and temptations by playing on the large range of issues connected with the division of Germany. She can, for instance, apply specific pressures in Berlin or make proposals on reunification negotiations or arms-control agreements in order to amplify existing differences in the West. (The way she has successfully used the proposed Non-Proliferation Treaty to strain relations among Western countries is a case in point.)

But West Germany remains the focus. Soviet leaders may still expect or desire that their actions will weaken the Federal Republic's ties to the West or that West German frustrations over her failure to make any progress on the issue of Germany's division may exhaust her rationality. It remains the specific objective of Soviet policy in Europe to destroy a corner-stone of the Western alliance, the American–German relationship which Brezhnev, at the Twenty-third Party Congress in 1966, denounced as the main danger to peace in Europe. But until that stage is reached, the Soviet Union can, as has been rightly

[72] Ibid.
[73] Brzezinski, p. 82.

observed, have her cake and eat it too; she can exploit the puta-
tive danger of a Western-supported German *revanchism* so as
to maintain control in Eastern Europe, and she can enjoy the
spectacle of the Federal Republic's annoyance with Britain,
France, and the United States, which she tries to amplify by
playing on latent Western fears of a resurgent Germany.[74]
Under these circumstances Soviet moves need not go beyond
the aim of consolidating the *status quo*; but once West Germany's estrangement from the West were sufficiently advanced,
the Russians could *then* become more expansionist, either by
applying pressures which the West might not be able to resist
as a body or by offering some kind of unification in exchange
for neutralization, which might well find attentive ears in
West Germany. This possibility leads us to the second ambiguity of Soviet policy: the uncertainty about whether to pursue
Soviet interests within the framework of a divided or a unified
Germany.

In his attempt to win control over all of Germany in the aftermath of the war, Stalin openly championed the unification of
Germany. Ironically, the French rather than the Russians
initially obstructed the implementation of the provisions of the
Potsdam Agreement that postulated unified administrative
structures for occupied Germany. In order to enlist support
from the German population, the Russians openly advocated
a central German government and instructed local Communists
to take a strong position in favour of national unity. The scope
of this essay does not permit a detailed examination of the
various Soviet moves in the early post-war years implementing
this policy,[75] but the reasons for its failure deserve brief scrutiny,
partly because they are still relevant.

Soviet policy simultaneously pursued incompatible objectives. Appeals to German nationalism and competition for
German allegiance were set against a policy of ruthless exploitation and brutal political oppression in the Soviet zone. Moreover, German public opinion was marked by anti-Soviet feelings
—some dating back to earlier years—and a traumatic fear of

[74] Hoffmann, *Gulliver's Troubles*, p. 436.
[75] On this point see Croan; see also Schwarz, *Vom Reich zur Bundesrepublik*,
pp. 203–69.

being overrun by Russia, and both these fears were reinforced by the Berlin blockade and later on by the Communist attack in Korea. Western policies offering at once security and rehabilitation were therefore far more attractive to the West Germans than Soviet appeals. And the Russians also did not find substantial support among the major political forces in the western part of Germany. The SPD, under Kurt Schumacher, though critical of specific policies of the Western Allies, was fundamentally pro-Western and anti-Communist and rejected any offer for collaboration proffered by the Communist Party. Finally, and in this respect both the Russians and the SPD, who had taken a staunchly nationalist line, erred in their assessment of political thinking in Germany; appeals to nationalism could hardly elicit a favourable response in a Germany that had entered an anti-nationalist phase and had found new meaning in the idea of European unity transcending the old nation-state.

The contradictory elements in Soviet policy continued even when the Soviet appeal for German unity was expressed in terms of a more flexible diplomacy, a phase that began with the 1952 note offering negotiations on neutralization. For the Russians simultaneously tightened the screws of authoritarian rule in their zone. According to all available evidence they were preparing a fresh initiative on the German question when the June 1953 uprising in East Germany drastically changed the picture, forcing the Russians to give support to Ulbricht, whose removal they had apparently begun to prepare.[76] Faced with a hardening Western attitude in the wake of the uprising, anything else would have seriously undermined the Soviet position in East Germany and Eastern Europe.

It is roughly from this moment on that Soviet policy became increasingly committed to strengthening the separate existence of the GDR, though it was only in 1955, on the occasion of West Germany's joining NATO, that this commitment was explicitly expressed. Rejecting four-power responsibility for reunification, the Soviet Union advocated unity through direct negotiations between 'the two German states' and backed the East German proposals for 'confederation'.

[76] See Arnulf Baring, *Der 17. Juni 1953* (1965) and Carola Stern, *Ulbricht; Eine politische Biographie* (1964), pp. 170–8.

The erection of the Berlin Wall in 1961 marked the beginning of a period in which Soviet pronouncements on the desirability of German unity have been conspicuously absent. Indeed, it was in March 1965 that Foreign Minister Gromyko made his assertion, mentioned earlier, namely that German unity might 'never' be achieved, because the two régimes had become too different. But it would be premature to conclude that Russia has written off for good the possibility of trying again to exploit the issue of German unity. A future offer to resume negotiations on unification, considered in the framework of some kind of neutralization for Germany, may well veil a new expansionist phase. It is true, as Pierre Hassner has noted in an excellent study, that in these two countries the idea of a new European security system has been explored more than elsewhere and that the search for it has more to do with political objectives than with security. But Soviet goals remain ambivalent, though 'it seems safe to assume that she will always tend to go for a bilateral deal with a partner whose collaboration she needs or whom she hopes to dominate, rather than for a collective-security framework which would put an end to alliances or spheres of influence'.[77]

What kept the Soviet Union from exploring the idea of German unity in the past and what may continue to keep her from doing so in the near future are the risks she runs if she seriously pursues this goal. Any solution on other than her own terms, *including* neutralization, implies concessions from *both* sides. The issues are inherently fluid and unpredictable, and, given the precariousness of the GDR's position and of the Soviet role in Eastern Europe, Russia may well prefer to postpone any move until it promises more certain benefits.

Before the conditions are ripe for a genuine Soviet proposal for a reunified and neutral Germany, Russia may well resort to the option I have mentioned before: the mere *offer* to negotiate neutralization in exchange for vague promises on unity could have disruptive consequences if West Germany's relations with the West have weakened and if, given the frustration arising from the failure to progress on the German divi-

[77] Pierre Hassner, 'Change and Security in Europe. Pt I: The Background', *Adelphi Paper*, no 45 (London, Inst. for Strategic Studies, 1968), p. 20.

sion, domestic forces which seek a short-cut to unity have gained the upper hand in the Federal Republic. In West Germany feelings on these issues are understandably very intense. The bitter domestic debates on rearmament, Western integration, and neutralization which shook the Federal Republic in the late 1940s and early 1950s testify to the strength of the emotions, amplified by feelings of insecurity, which these issues can evoke. New conflicts between different factions, advocating variations of a firm Western course or neutrality, would seriously strain the political structure of the Federal Republic. Moreover, a Soviet proposal would cause strenuous debates in the West, widen present differences of policy, and endanger existing institutions and patterns of co-operation. Most dangerous to the Federal Republic, it could lead to her isolation from other Western powers.

Thus, despite increasing willingness in the Federal Republic to try new policies and despite some strains in her relations with the Western powers, from the Soviet point of view, the situation is still far from being developed enough to make this option worth while. Whether or not the situation in Germany and Europe does deteriorate to the point where Soviet initiatives can be expected depends partly on how the Western Allies handle Germany's goal of unity, and it is this problem to which we shall now turn.

Reunification as a common goal: a necessity for the West?

If the West has powerful reasons for opposing German unity, why should it then be interested in supporting the Federal Republic's main foreign-policy objective of reunification? Even to *raise* the issue seriously, not just in a declaratory way, calls into question the continuation of NATO, European integration, and other frameworks of co-operation in the West, just as it calls into question parallel institutions in the East. Almost all Western powers fear the uncertain consequences of change with regard to Germany. In the face of the arguments against German reunification, can a case be made *for* Western support of German unity in terms of the Western countries' own self-interest?

Some voices in Western public opinion—heard more fre-

quently in Britain than elsewhere among the major powers—
have urged on West Germany and the West as a whole a policy
of accepting the German division as final, and have argued with
increasing impatience that the Federal Republic's pursuance of
unity is a futile revolt against history's verdict, if not an outright threat to peace. But this argument underestimates the
disruptive consequences for Germany and Europe if the West
were to abandon support for what the Germans continue to regard as their most important objective.

What might happen if the West were to stop supporting
German unity? Obviously, there would be little immediate
consequence as far as the *division* of Germany is concerned,
since whether the West gives support to unity or none at all,
the present state of Europe's division is not likely to change
drastically in the near future. But with regard to the Federal
Republic's relations with the West and her internal stability,
abandonment of support for her main foreign-policy objective
will very likely have disastrous consequences, for such a step
would break a pledge made repeatedly to Bonn in international
treaties and Western policy, and inevitably undercut those
political forces in the Federal Republic which justified a firm
course of reconciliation and integration with the West by arguing that their policy would serve the national interest of unity.
Such a change of Western policy towards a country which tried
hard to be a loyal ally would probably cause deep resentment
and undermine the Federal Republic's relations with the West
as well as the existing framework of co-operation. Simultaneously such a development would activate West Germany's
deep sense of insecurity and isolation trauma referred to above.

But, more important, the West has a long-term interest in
somehow alleviating the German division. If a *détente* is to lead
to a lasting European settlement, it is hardly conceivable that
such a process could avoid the heart of the continent. This is all
the more true because of the intensive interaction between a
strategically located Germany and the international system as a
whole. This assessment is, however, not to be confused with the
assertion once made by West German policy-makers that reunification was a *prerequisite* to a *détente*. Whatever the logic
and purpose of this position, events of the last years have

demonstrated that a relaxation of tension can *begin* without reunification. But it will remain impossible for a *détente* to create a better and stable order in Europe unless the problem of Germany is solved.

The West's interest in supporting the long-term objective of German unity is equally pertinent to another area. It results from a simple and puzzling paradox: if the Western powers prefer West Germany to remain a junior partner dependent on them for the realization of her main national goal, then by necessity they must support this goal of unity about which most of them have serious reservations.

Despite her significant economic and demographic resources, the Federal Republic has been comparatively less influential on the crucial diplomatic and military issues of East–West relations. As we have seen, this special position has two origins. In the first place it results from the German defeat in World War II. Germany's sovereignty was only partially restored. In the second place, however, the restriction of the Federal Republic's sovereignty was not only imposed, but also voluntarily accepted and observed. Germany's junior role and the assumption by the Allies of major responsibilities over West Germany's future was—as we have also seen—one of the German contributions to what we have earlier called the 'package deal' between the nascent Bonn Republic and the Western powers. As Article 2 of the 1954 Convention on the Relations between Three Powers and the Federal Republic of Germany stipulates:

In view of the international situation, which has so far prevented the reunification of Germany and the conclusion of a peace settlement, the Three Powers retain the rights and the responsibilities heretofore exercised or held by them relating to Berlin and to Germany as a whole, including the reunification of Germany and a peace settlement.

Moreover, other agreements concluded on the same occasion restrict or prohibit production of certain arms, such as nuclear weapons. It is important to note (and is often overlooked) that the Soviet Union in her Treaty of Friendship with East Germany of June 1964, reiterated her sovereign prerogatives in Germany by stating in Article 9: 'This Treaty does not affect the rights and obligations resulting for both parties from other bilateral and international agreements including the Potsdam Agreement.'

The collapse of the Third Reich will soon be a generation removed, and the two-thirds of the German population that were unborn or were children in 1945 are at present less responsive than their elders to the burdens of a legacy for which they do not feel responsible. Therefore the clauses limiting German sovereignty may continue to be legally binding, but they lose the moral and political weight that originally derived from the Germans' defeat and sense of guilt.

However, the matter is a different one if we turn to the second rationale for assigning Germany a special status. As long as reunification and the freedom of Berlin remain the prime objectives of German foreign policy, the Federal Republic has a meaningful incentive to accept a secondary status within the Western system, provided she receives in return the indispensable support for reunification from her allies. Because of its constructive purpose such a limitation is acceptable to all sectors of the domestic political spectrum, and under such circumstances the Federal Republic is not likely to question this special status even if the legacy of defeat were to lose some of its meaning. She knows that the German problem cannot be solved without their help. The implications of this particular connexion have always been better understood by the French under de Gaulle than by the British. The sympathetic support that France has given to Germany's main objective makes sense in the context not only of de Gaulle's vision of a reunited Europe but also of French national interests, for it preserves a distance between France and a Germany which would have to content herself with the role of a junior partner at the side of a France whose policy takes into account and promotes German interests.

If France (or Britain for that matter) wants to eliminate Germany as a rival for leadership in Europe or simply as a power that could use its resources to play a more prominent role in this area, she almost *has* to support German unity.[78] (As

[78] For a different but stimulating interpretation, see John Newhouse, *Collision in Brussels: The Common Market Crisis of 30 June 1965* (1967), pp. 151–85.

we shall see later, such support has been made less costly by treating German reunification as the product of a historical process of European reunification.) Of course, this logic can be reversed: the Federal Republic can use her continued acceptance of a secondary status to put pressure on her allies to support her in overcoming the division.

Therefore, abandonment by the United States, France, or Britain of support for reunification as a long-term objective of the West could raise more problems than it solves. Such a step would throw Germany back on her own resources for autonomous action. But since these are extremely limited she would probably feel obliged to maximize them by discarding the previously accepted limitations of sovereignty for which she would no longer get the desired support in return.

West Germany's post-war foreign policy, as Alfred Grosser has rightly pointed out, has been characterized by a refusal to think in global terms. She has withdrawn from wider ambitions and, with a certain 'Germanocentrism', tends to see every issue of international politics in the light of the German division.[79] But this state of affairs points to a dynamic potential in Western policy: a continuation of support for German unity offers incentives and a constructive framework within which German interests can find satisfaction without necessarily blocking a policy of movement in Europe.

But, to return to the paradox referred to earlier, *how* can the Western powers support the objective of German unity which many of them are not eager to see realized? One, by no means unpopular, way out of the dilemma would be to beg the issue. Since progress towards German reunification is difficult and improbable in the near future, endorsement of the general objective costs little. Hoping that support of German unity can be confined to verbal promise without ever being obliged to deliver the goods, and that reunification remains out of practical reach, the temptation is great to reconcile through mere lip service the need to support the Federal Republic with reservations about eventual German unity.

Although expedient now, in the long run this stand is likely to be counterproductive. Not only would it be difficult to con-

[79] Grosser, *Die Bundesrepublik*, pp. 57 ff.

ceal real intentions over a long period of time; but if and when the growing consensus among Western countries to overcome the division of Europe through a new security system and 'peaceful engagement' leads to more sweeping action than the present bilateral involvement in Eastern Europe, it will be difficult to continue hiding behind verbal formulas, since such initiatives would have to extend to the problems of divided Germany. From that moment onward the Western governments would have to elaborate and bring into the open their opinions and intentions concerning a solution of the problem.

But the need to resort to window-dressing techniques has decreased. Though Western governments may still have misgivings about the option of reuniting Germany into a new version of a strong Reich, support of eventual unification has become easier because the whole concept of a unified Germany has changed. The Germans themselves have begun to reassess the possible shape and purpose of unity and alternative strategies of achieving it. As we shall see, the reassessments attempt to cope with the objections and reservations which have been at the basis of non-German concern about the potential consequences of reunification. For this reason, the gulf that in the past separated the views of non-Germans and Germans on a number of issues is beginning to be bridged. And the reassessment of German policy on reunification is changing some of the basic premises upon which the future evolution of East–West relations in Europe will be based. With these points in mind, let us focus our analysis on the changing priorities of the *Deutschlandpolitik* in the Federal Republic.

6

THE EVOLUTION OF A NEW FOREIGN POLICY
FOR THE FEDERAL REPUBLIC

THE changes in the international system of the Cold War have had a profound impact on the reunification policy which the Federal Republic had pursued since her foundation. As a result every single major ingredient of that policy has been either fundamentally altered or significantly modified in the recent past. The 'turn in the German problem', referred to in the opening section of this essay, is therefore the most visible and probably the most momentous in West Germany's policy on German unity.

How has the *Deutschlandpolitik* of the Federal Republic changed? Let us first briefly define the main components of German reunification policy and how they have been altered. Post-war policy can be subsumed under six (simplified) major tenets:[80]

1. Unity was to be achieved through an elimination of Communist rule in East Germany in the near future, either by free elections or overthrow from within and the subsequent establishment of all-German institutions. This tenet has been radically changed. Institutional unity is no longer at the centre of the reunification concept, but, rather, the preservation of the nation's common heritage and the improvement of political conditions in East Germany—achieved by a long historical process which may ultimately end in institutional unity as well. But the shape of the institutions cannot be determined in advance.

2. Since the government of the Federal Republic was freely elected and the GDR government was not, only the former was entitled to speak in the name of *all* Germans, including those living under the Communist régime (*Alleinvertretungsanspruch*). This policy began to change with the establishment of diplomatic relations with Rumania in 1967, when for the

---

[80] For a forceful presentation of Bonn's *Deutschlandpolitik* in the first decade, see Wilhelm G. Grewe, *Deutsche Aussenpolitik der Nachkriegszeit* (1960); Ernst Majonica, *Deutsche Aussenpolitik* (1965).

first time Germany was represented by two governments in a country outside the Soviet Union, thus weakening by implication Bonn's claim to be the sole legal representative of all of Germany. The West German government realized that the rigid maintenance of this claim would not only make the dialogue it hoped to establish with East Berlin difficult, but would also hinder establishment of relations with the East European governments, which were under strong pressure from the GDR to reject this 'insolent' claim to speak for the East Germans.

3. Until reunification, and in order not to preclude it, the Communist régime was not to be recognized or made party to official contacts but, on the contrary, to be ostracized wherever possible. This policy was significantly altered in favour of a 'live and let live' attitude, with Chancellor Kiesinger exchanging messages with Premier Stoph, and West German government members assuring the East German authorities that they did not seek their overthrow.

4. In order to keep the Communist régime isolated and to prevent international recognition of Germany's division, the Federal Republic refused to have diplomatic relations with governments recognizing the GDR, except for the Soviet Union (the Hallstein Doctrine). This policy has been partially revised, beginning under the Erhard government, and continued by the Great Coalition. The revision was limited to relations with the Communist régimes in Europe, Rumania being the first and Yugoslavia the second country where the new policy bore fruit.

5. The borders of a reunited Germany would remain provisional until settlement at a final peace conference. The Great Coalition has made a formal concession only *vis-à-vis* Czechoslovakia, by declaring the Munich Agreement invalid, but not on the Oder–Neisse issue. Nevertheless, German policy has shown signs of compromise, implying the future possibility of German concessions in exchange for progress in overcoming the division.

6. Finally, while German reunification remained the obligation and responsibility of the four great powers, if a relaxation of tension was to be sought by the West, reunification was to be its prerequisite. This tenet, which was so to speak a safety

device in case the 'policy of strength' failed, has been reversed entirely. It is now held by the new German government that unity can only come as the *consequence* of a relaxation of tensions. The best German contribution to reunification, therefore, consists in supporting a *détente* through active diplomacy.

Having thus summarized the changes which have occurred in German foreign policy on reunification, we turn to a closer analysis of the modifications of its components. But before we do so we must take a look at the original shape of German policy and how it came to change.

The old policy in a changing environment

These various components in the Federal Republic's policy on German unity were fairly consistent, not only in themselves but also *vis-à-vis* policy on the Western Alliance. Unequivocal option for the West as well as participation in European integration and Western co-operation and defence efforts were the counterparts to the Eastern dimension of her foreign policy. Moreover, on each of the major tenets of German policy on reunification, the Western powers gave the Federal Republic their full and explicit support.

West Germany's aim to eliminate the Communist régime in East Germany was no more than one intra-German aspect of the Cold War. After all, it had been in the atmosphere created by the Berlin blockade that West German political leaders had made the crucial decision to establish the Federal Republic. Their reunification proposals—always with free elections as their central element—reflected the view that a 'policy of strength' would sooner or later lead to a breakdown of communism in Central and Eastern Europe, and aimed at the victory of the Western system of government in East Germany, which would then automatically ensure reunification. From this basic position stemmed, first, the refusal to accept, recognize, or deal with the East German Communist government, second, the Hallstein Doctrine, designed to isolate the régime and prevent international recognition of the division, and, finally, the refusal to recognize the territorial *status quo* as final; this was regarded as a dangerous and unnecessary concession.

It was consistent with this policy to abstain from political involvement in the Communist world and to confine West Germany's role to active participation on the anti-Communist front. The establishment of diplomatic relations with Moscow was an exception (and was done despite misgivings among the Western Allies). It was absolutely crucial to prevent both the *status quo* of the division of Germany from becoming permanent and the attempted improvements in East–West relations from bypassing Germany. Bonn's assertion that Germany's division was the main source of tension in Europe and that consequently German reunification was a prerequisite for a *détente* followed logically from the basic policy premise. But that also meant that the West Germans always had to remind the Allies of the German problem whenever the latter explored new possibilities for lowering tension with the Communist world.

The increase in momentum of those international forces which sought to overcome the Cold War only strengthened the West German politicians' fears that Germany's division might indeed become final. As a result, West German leaders insisted even more adamantly that the division itself was still the main source of tension—and they did so for several reasons. If Germany's division was no longer regarded as the major European problem, non-Germans might lose interest in eliminating it. Reminders and frequent references to incidents of violence at the Berlin Wall or along the Iron Curtain emphasized its existence and importance. It was also necessary to appease the rising fear within West Germany that, in a world where old dividing lines were breaking down, increasingly successful efforts to achieve *détente* might bypass Germany altogether. Germany's 'coalition nightmare' of the Bismarck period and after thus reappeared as a fear of *Einkreisung* (encirclement) or of bilateral deals between a Western ally and the Soviet Union at Germany's expense, particularly during the later part of the Adenauer administration. Britain's independent initiatives towards Moscow, and de Gaulle's growing involvement in Eastern Europe intensified German apprehensions.

As the pressure for a relaxation grew stronger, the Western Allies viewed West Germany's efforts to keep the German question open with less and less sympathy. By the early 1960s, particularly after Kennedy's election, to many political leaders in the West a policy whose logic was based on challenging the East and whose success depended on a *victory* of the West appeared (though it had once been their own) as a burdensome obstacle to progress. In particular the kind of institutional unity sought by the Federal Republic seemed more unrealizable than ever; to treat reunification as the prerequisite to a *détente* was therefore bound to look like obstruction to a relaxation of tension. The change in perspective was even more radical with regard to West Germany's policy on the borders: the rejection of the territorial *status quo*, once meaningful (and supported by the West), now appeared like a threat to peace and an obstacle to an East–West rapprochement.

Even the weaker and subtler West German attempts to prevent the hardening of the *status quo* began to be perceived by other countries as hindrances to East–West relaxation. Typical of such efforts were the activities of the *Kuratorium Unteilbares Deutschland* (Council for an Indivisible Germany), a non-partisan and government-supported institution whose tasks President Lübke defined in December 1964 as: 'To be a guardian against all temptations to become accustomed to the *status quo* of the division of our people', and to maintain a 'salutary unrest' about Germany's division.[81] This objective had been formulated more forcefully in 1963 by Johann Gradl, then a CDU Deputy from Berlin and later Minister for Refugees and Expellees in the Erhard government. 'We therefore must try to become tactfully impatient and get on people's nerves. Tactfully means in particular without force, but with pressure and demands at every opportunity.'[82]

Similarly, Bonn's policy towards the East German government became increasingly unprofitable in the late 1950s and early 1960s. Refusal to have contacts with the Communist régime on the grounds that this would amount to a recognition of the GDR—and thereby to a renunciation of West Germany's intention of reunification—made sense as long as (1) a Soviet refusal to permit reunification was uncertain; (2) the East

[81] *Bulletin*, 9 Dec. 1964.
[82] Johann Baptist Gradl, 'Ist Wiedervereinigung aktuell?' in H. A. Jacobsen and O. Stenzl, eds., *Deutschland und die Welt* (1964), p. 211.

German régime seemed on the brink of collapse; and (3) the reconstitution of all-German institutions was considered the most urgent goal and one that could be reached in the near future. But Soviet policy began to give every impression that early reunification was ruled out. The East German régime was steadily gaining strength,[83] and the anti-Communist struggle which was intended to make possible German unity in the form of common institutions had been replaced by efforts to decrease East–West tensions.

Within West Germany, Bonn's policy began to be assailed on the grounds that by rejecting all measures that did not lead to the *status quo ante bellum* (World War II), the Federal Republic condemned herself to protracted inaction and contributed to sharpening the division until the point where the dissimilarities and antagonisms between the two German countries put reunification out of the question. The policy had led, the domestic critics argued, to a 'recognition psychosis' such that the Federal Republic had repeatedly neglected opportunities to maintain or revive links with the other part of Germany.[84] West German policy was in a dilemma: would dealings with East Berlin lead to a recognition of the division or—if I may be allowed to quote from an article I wrote at that time—'could a policy of rejecting intra-German contacts amount to a *de facto* recognition of Germany's partition since the division deepens every year?'[85]

Though the changes in West German policy occurred only

[83] Two studies substantiated this point at a crucial moment in the evolution of West German opinion, the first an account of a visit, the second an academic study: Marion Gräfin Dönhoff, Rudolf Walter Leonhardt, Theo Sommer, *Reise in ein fernes Land* (1964); Ernst Richert, *Das Zweite Deutschland*. For a sociological survey see Peter Christian Ludz, ed., *Studien und Materialien zur Soziologie der DDR*, special issue of *Kölner Zeitschrift für Soziologie und Sozialpsychologie*, no. 78 (Cologne, 1964); see also two interpretative essays: Ralf Dahrendorf, *Society and Democracy in Germany* (1967), pp. 419–50; Jean Edward Smith, 'The Red Prussianism of the German Democratic Republic', *Political Science Quarterly*, Sept. 1967, pp. 368–85; for a journalistic study with debatable conclusions see Welles Hangen, *The Muted Revolution* (1966).

[84] The self-imposed limitations of Bonn's policy could be observed, for instance, when during the summer of 1963 an attempt to arrange an exchange of newspapers to be sold publicly in both parts of Germany was blocked by the West German law which prohibits the importation of Communist literature. The Great Coalition subsequently tried to clear the way for it, but at the time of writing it is uncertain whether East Berlin will pursue the West German offer.

[85] Kaiser, *Frankfurter Hefte*, Jan. 1966, p. 41.

in the 1960s, the historical forces that created them had their origin in earlier years. The relaxation of tension and the consolidation of the Communist régimes began already in the 1950s. Still, three developments of the 1960s are particularly important in the evolution of West German thinking and policy: the building of the Berlin Wall in 1961 and subsequent efforts to re-establish some freedom of movement in the divided city, the *détente* policies of the Kennedy Administration and Bonn's overtures towards Eastern Europe and, finally, de Gaulle's proposals and policy to overcome the division of Europe and Germany.

The Berlin Wall and domestic priorities: institutional unity *versus* humanitarian concerns

On that fateful week-end of 13 August 1961, when the Communist authorities in one swift move erected the Berlin Wall, more happened than the closing of a last escape route to the West. Berlin, with its relatively unrestricted contact between the two parts of Germany, was the last remnant of a once-united Germany. The open city was a threat to the survival of the Communist economy and a tremendous challenge to the East German régime. It had become a symbol for the unsettled and open character of the German problem and was the last refuge of old hopes that the tide of history could still change in favour of German unity through a victory of Western institutions and government. When the Berlin Wall was erected, with little more than verbal protest from the Western Allies, several points became obvious to the Germans. First, the 'policy of strength' had failed in its offensive goals and promises; second, the Communist régime in East Germany could not be made to collapse in the near future and was here to stay; finally, the international system of the northern hemisphere *had* crystallized whether one liked it or not, around the partition into two zones of influence of Europe and of Germany; this structure had some permanency and could not soon be expected to change drastically.

For the first time since the great debate between opposition and government in the late 1940s and early 1950s the fundamental direction and ultimate purpose of West German foreign policy were reappraised. Indeed, the most important contributions to the debate that shaped German thinking and subsequent policy changes were made *post murum*. (The only notable exception was Karl Jaspers' provocative proposal in 1960, to which we shall return.) The erection of the Berlin Wall was a decisive turning point in the history of the Federal Republic.

Since the events of 1961 made it clear that unity could not be realized in the near future, the heart of Bonn's reunification policy, the establishment of common (Western) institutions, automatically lost all pertinence. Domestic critics now raised the question whether, rather than making the reconstitution of common institutions West Germany's most immediate concern, she should instead give priority to the creation of more tolerable living conditions in East Germany and a liberalization of her régime, while trying simultaneously to revive or maintain intra-German cohesion. It had long been held in the Federal Republic that only German unity could bring freedom to the East Germans. Though this was undoubtedly true (if unity was achieved on Western terms), critics now argued that this was simply not the real issue, as long as the Soviet Union refused to allow the formation of a reunited 'Western' Germany. If the liberalization of East Germany depended on reunification, neither development was attainable.

The demand for a change of Bonn's priority had first been provocatively formulated by Karl Jaspers in 1960, when he suggested that the Federal Republic should renounce her primary demand for unity if in exchange freedom could be gained for the East Germans.[86] His proposals encountered vehement opposition and initiated a lively debate. All three major political parties rejected them, although similar suggestions had actually appeared in several official statements. During a Bundestag debate on 20 March 1958 Chancellor Adenauer had remarked, 'I am concerned that we should finally reach the point where the 17 million Germans behind the Iron Curtain can live as they wish. Therefore, I think we should view this whole question not in national, nationalistic, or power perspectives, but from the point of view of the constraints to which 17 million

---

[86] He developed them further and published them later in Jaspers, *Lebensfragen der deutschen Politik* (1963).

Germans have been submitted, namely, to a way of life and thinking which they do not want.' Defence Minister Strauss had made a similar statement in the same debate, and Adenauer reiterated it in October 1962.[87] According to Adenauer's memoirs the Chancellor even tried twice in conversations with the Soviet ambassador to Bonn and Deputy Prime Minister Mikoyan in March and April 1958 to sound out Soviet interests in an 'Austrian solution' for East Germany, thus focusing on the living conditions of the East Germans rather than institutional unity, but the Soviet leaders did not respond and Khrushchev's Berlin ultimatum of the same year closed the matter.[88] Therefore the statements quoted above remained isolated hints of alternative priorities which did not become official policy. Nevertheless, Jaspers' main theme was taken up by others, developed further, and subsequently never entirely disappeared from the forefront of public debate until it became official policy in 1966-7.

Another factor gave further momentum to the debate on priorities and carried it into the realm of alternative strategies: the issue of pass agreements in Berlin. After the Wall was built, the East Germans prohibited any movement of East or West Berliners across the new frontier. Ever since, the city government of West Berlin has repeatedly offered to negotiate about an easement of the ban, particularly for special occasions such as Christmas. But its initiatives were unsuccessful until the winter of 1963, when the government of the GDR—not the East Berlin city administration—responded favourably. After fairly short negotiations, the two sides agreed to issue passes to West Berliners to visit relatives in East Berlin between 18 December 1963 and 5 January 1964. Negotiations had been opened with a message from the Deputy Prime Minister of the GDR to the Mayor of West Berlin, and they were conducted by an East German Under-Secretary of State and a high official of the West Berlin city administration. These two in-

---

[87] Adenauer then suggested that humanitarian considerations were more important than national ones, and that the German government was willing to talk about 'a lot of things' if only some self-determination could be achieved in East Germany. Text in Heinrich von Siegler, *Wiedervereinigung und Sicherheit Deutschlands* (1964), p. 261.

[88] Konrad Adenauer, *Erinnerungen, 1955-9*, vol. iii. (1967), pp. 369-96.

stitutions acted as the parties to the protocol on 'passes for inhabitants of Berlin (West) to visit relatives in Berlin (East)/ Capital of the GDR' and their representatives signed it.[89]

This accord soon became the subject of domestic controversy in West Germany, notably on the grounds that direct negotiations with the East German government could be interpreted as a step towards recognition of it. To mention East Berlin as 'the capital of the GDR' in an official document signed by Western representatives had no precedent. Moreover, so the critics argued, since the West Berlin city administration did not negotiate with its Eastern counterpart, the Communist claim that West Berlin should be treated as a political entity of its own, separate from the Federal Republic, had implicitly been accepted. And indeed, the East Germans stressed both points in their propaganda efforts exploiting the pass agreement.[90] Thus, in view of the Communist tactics to undermine Western influence in West Berlin and to use the Berlin issue for the larger purpose of disrupting the Western Alliance, the criticism was not entirely unfounded.[91]

Events connected with the pass agreement exposed and aggravated political differences between the Bonn and West Berlin administrations which had been developing ever since the erection of the Wall.[92] For it was in Berlin that the failure of past Western and German policy to make progress in overcoming the division was most immediately felt. The ugly reality of the Wall, the shootings there, the ever-felt presence of a hostile environment, and the frustration in the wake of repeated failure to approach successfully the East Berlin authorities on the premises of the old policies, provided the context for Berlin's fundamental rethinking of the earlier *Deutschlandpolitik*. Bahr's proposals for a more pragmatic policy towards

[89] For the text of the protocol and a brief analysis of the negotiations and ensuing controversies, see Gottfried Vetter, 'Passierscheine in Deutschland', *Europa-Archiv*, May 1964, pp. 305–18.

[90] See, e.g., *Neues Deutschland*, 18 Dec. 1963.

[91] The scope of this essay does not permit us to examine this agreement in the light of Berlin's strategic position. For further reading on this subject, see works by Henry A. Kissinger, John Mander, James L. Richardson, Jean E. Smith, Hans Speier, and Philip Windsor, listed in bibliography.

[92] On this aspect see Kurt L. Shell, *Bedrohung und Bewährung. Führung und Bevölkerung in der Berliner Krise* (1966).

East Berlin, to which we shall refer later, are an example of this rethinking, and they reflected a widespread malaise that was shared even by many of those Berliners who disagreed with his specific proposals. Mayor Brandt—who, like many members of the Berlin Social Democrats, was receptive to Kennedy's ideas about improving relations with the Communist world—began to move towards a more flexible policy and advocated a more forceful West German contribution to *détente*, at a time when the Bonn government under Adenauer and then Erhard was still reluctant to abandon essential elements of the 'policy of strength'.[93]

It was in the context of divided Berlin where the humanitarian concerns—in this case with regard to reuniting separated families—for the first time clashed on the level of political decision (and not of mere debate) with the *raison d'état* of Bonn's policy on the division. Since East Berlin had been adamant for two years in its demands to have negotiations on passes take place between the GDR and West Berlin, it can be reasonably assumed that authorities in the Western part of the divided city knew their efforts would be unsuccessful until they conceded this and the other points mentioned earlier. Therefore, both supporters and critics of the pass agreement had substantial evidence to support their case. The former could point to the concrete humanitarian benefits of a new approach to East Germany, and the latter could argue that East Berlin had used humanitarian concerns in the West to blackmail the West, since the political costs far outweighed the returns. Where would the road lead if every pass agreement had to be bought with further concessions?[94]

The government in Bonn was sceptical, to say the least, about the widsom of the Berlin administration's approach, and raised a number of objections during the negotiations of 1963 and the following years, which the Berlin negotiators often resented as unnecessary interference. Brandt, whose re-

---

[93] See Willy Brandt's Harvard lectures, 1962, *The Ordeal of Coexistence* (1963).

[94] The protocol referred to the remaining disagreements among the negotiators in two sentences: 'Notwithstanding the differing political and legal points of view, the two sides were guided by the opinion that it should be possible to carry out this humanitarian task. Both sides notify that they could not agree on common terms on places, institutions, and functions'. Vetter, *Europa-Archiv*, May 1964, p. 313.

lationship with the CDU–FDP government was complicated at that time by his position as the opposition's candidate for Chancellor, had a difficult course to steer. On the one hand he had to achieve a sufficient degree of independence from Bonn to be able to explore new policies on Berlin issues, and, on the other, he had to maintain enough loyalty to the Federal Government to be sure of keeping its still indispensable backing.

Brandt's policy on the pass-agreement issue had two consequences. First, by applying new priorities it brought about small but real changes in intra-German relations *within the context of Berlin*. As we shall see below, some of them anticipated later moves by the Great Coalition. Second, it stirred up the West German debate on the future of Bonn's *Deutschlandpolitik*, creating new divisions, and polarizing it around issues raised in Berlin. The Bonn government, though apprehensive about the consequences of the Mayor of Berlin's action, felt compelled to recognize the pressure of public opinion—itself divided but on the whole favourable—and of supporters of the Berlin administration in its own ranks. Not only did the FDP back the pass agreement, but some Christian Democrat members of the cabinet did too, who thought that humanitarian concerns should take precedence over some of the tenets of the old policy of strength and isolation *vis-à-vis* the GDR.

Ferments of change: Kennedy's policy and Bonn's *Ostpolitik*

Public discussion about the future of Germany soon moved from the plane of priorities to that of political strategies. A crucial factor in producing this shift was the advent of the Kennedy Administration with its new policy. Many of its major tenets had a direct bearing on West German policy: its scrapping of the old Manichean Cold War concepts, its search for a new global role for the United States as a promoter and guardian of peace, its acknowledgement that the *status quo* could not change radically in a nuclear world. Though firm in the face of Soviet expansion, Kennedy nevertheless attempted to establish a new relationship with the Soviet Union by singling out areas of common concern where both countries could co-operate in the interest of world stability.

D

Kennedy's 'strategy for peace' was not specifically designed to solve the problems of Europe or Germany—an absolutely crucial difference from de Gaulle's—but was global in scope. The Federal Republic, like all the other allies of the United States, was only assigned an auxiliary role in contributing to and sharing the burdens of the American attempt to achieve *détente*—a policy whose priorities reflected Kennedy's sense of the bipolar structure of world politics. If Germany's interests were to be satisfied, it would occur indirectly through a success of this wider strategy. Simultaneously, however, Kennedy's policy by implication scrapped almost all of the major tenets of Bonn's former *Deutschlandpolitik*. This dual consequence of American policy explains its strong impact on both public opinion and governmental policy in West Germany.

Kennedy's policy had a twofold effect on the German government. First, it naturally caused strains in American–West German relations. But, considering that American policy by implication put in question several essential elements of Adenauer's post-war foreign policy, these strains were fairly limited, partly, no doubt, because of Bonn's dependence on Washington. (But these frictions also contributed to changes in West German attitudes, eventually leading to the different and more assertive position *vis-à-vis* the United States that was assumed under the Great Coalition.) To Kennedy, Adenauer's reminders about the German problem, and American pledges of support seemed to be increasingly burdensome attempts to tie him to outdated policies which would obstruct progress on global strategies of *détente*. Conversely, Adenauer began to fear that American policy might sacrifice German and European interests in its attempt to reach agreement with the Soviet Union, a fear that was shared by a large sector of the German public.

But American policy at the same time struck a responsive chord in the West German government. In fact, Washington strengthened already existing tendencies in Bonn. Kennedy's 'strategy for peace' (and, later, Johnson's proposals for 'bridge-building' and 'peaceful engagement') stressed the importance of more dealings with the Communist world. Under Foreign Minister Gerhard Schröder, the *Auswärtiges Amt* (Foreign

Office) quietly pursued that very goal: trade missions in Poland, Hungary, Bulgaria, and Rumania were the first stages of a reactivated *Ostpolitik*, the next objectives of which were the establishment of consular and diplomatic relations. Indeed, Schröder cautiously began to follow the critics of Bonn's Eastern policy and accepted the idea of not applying the Hallstein Doctrine to Eastern Europe. (The establishment of diplomatic relations was negotiated with Rumania during 1966, though Bonn was not able to put into effect the agreement until after the formation of the Great Coalition.)

Bonn's renewed *Ostpolitik* in the closing days of the Adenauer government and under Erhard was ambiguous, however, because its objectives were only removed, not dissociated, from the older Cold War policies. For this reason, Schröder's Eastern policy, strictly speaking, only prepared the ground for but was not an earlier version of the policy of the Great Coalition, where it became part of a revised foreign policy of *détente*. The rationale of Schröder's policy was similar to certain ideas behind Brzezinski's proposals for a 'peaceful engagement',[95] which found sympathetic ears in West German government circles and the CDU at that time: through the West's involvement in Eastern Europe, it was thought that the division of the continent might gradually be overcome. But East Germany had to be excluded, systematically ostracized, and preserved as a political anachronism. With a growing East–West *détente*, it would then become increasingly dispensable, and finally a burden, at which point the Communist countries might release it. Thus, the reunification of Europe would lead to the reunification of Germany.

However, the connexion between these views and Bonn's involvement in Eastern Europe should not be overemphasized. But some elements in Brzezinski's proposals which, not surprisingly, also drew some criticism in Germany,[96] were apparent in German policy. Also, closer relations with the East European countries were viewed as a means of building a better basis for Bonn's claim to represent all of Germany and to

[95] See Brzezinski, *Alternative to Partition*.
[96] Notably Peter Bender, 'Die DDR nicht isolieren', in Theo Sommer, ed., *Denken an Deutschland* (1966).

challenge and isolate the GDR. And, since the Federal Republic still adhered to her earlier position in other areas of her
foreign policy, the ulterior motives of her activities in Eastern
Europe seemed questionable to the Communist countries.

Moscow suspected that West Germany was out to undermine its influence in Eastern Europe. Soviet leaders could
hardly have forgotten that only a few years earlier anti-Communist and anti-Russian militancy had been an essential part
of Bonn's policy. The Federal Republic's 'Peace Note' of
March 1966, though making several conciliatory gestures towards the East, and though intended to make a German contribution to the relaxation of tensions, denounced the threatening
character of Soviet policy in a passage that could well have been
written at the height of the Cold War. And the other European
Communist countries must have viewed Bonn's diplomatic
offensive with mixed feelings. Whatever the differences between them, they had to make sure that Bonn's objective in
establishing relations with them of isolating and challenging
the GDR would not damage their *own* relations with East
Germany, who was after all a socialist ally. Equally important,
as long as the Federal Republic's Eastern policy had under-
tones of hostility to the Soviet Union, and as long as Russia
was apprehensive about West Germany's involvement in
Eastern Europe, their margin of manoeuvre in responding to
Bonn's initiatives was limited.

Schröder's active *Ostpolitik* never realized its original objectives. It could not have done so, given the limitations imposed
by the orthodoxy of the rest of Bonn's foreign policy and the
strength of domestic obstruction. As Roger Morgan has shown
in greater detail, obstruction did not come from the opposition
party but from the conservative forces within the CDU/CSU.[97]
For example in 1966 they vetoed within the cabinet a decision
to establish relations with Rumania, although the Foreign
Office had cleared the way in negotiations with Bucharest;
they were also responsible for some last-minute insertions into
the 'Peace Note' which contradicted the rest of the document,
such as the reference to the 1937 borders. Chancellor Erhard's

[97] Roger Morgan, 'The Scope of German Foreign Policy', *The Yearbook of World Affairs, 1966*, pp. 78–105.

weak position was another obstacle to a new approach, for strong leadership would have been necessary to overcome opposition in his own party and the cabinet. For this reason hints and offers from Prague during the spring of 1966 to consider the establishment of diplomatic relations were not followed up for fear of offending the supporters of the Hallstein Doctrine.

Still, the more active Eastern policy under Schröder did score *some* successes. It made the Federal Republic re-enter Central and Eastern Europe at an official level. But, more important, it represented the first *significant* departure from Bonn's post-war foreign policy and naturally affected its other components, ultimately calling into question its entire structure. This can be summed up as follows:

If Bonn's desire to engage peacefully in Eastern Europe was to be credible, a rigid position on the border problem became untenable—hence, pressure to be more conciliatory on the frontier issues.

If the diplomatic offensive was to lead to diplomatic relations, the Hallstein Doctrine could not be maintained, and two German governments would have to be represented in the East European capitals—hence the necessity to revise this tenet and by implication to undermine (despite solemn declarations to the contrary) Bonn's previous claim to represent all of Germany, the *Alleinvertretungsanspruch.*

If the Federal Republic was to open diplomatic relations with Communist countries that were and had to be responsive to pressures from the GDR (with regard to the recognition of two German states), she would carry the ferment of change into her intra-German policy—hence, pressure to consummate *within* Germany the change she had already accepted outside.

Most important, if Bonn's objective to engage peacefully in Eastern Europe was to be both meaningful to the Germans and credible on both sides of the Iron Curtain, Cold War postures no longer made sense—hence the need to reverse the Bonn position and treat the reunification of Germany no longer as a prerequisite but as a result of a relaxation of tension to which the Federal Republic would be called to contribute.

A partial withdrawal from West Germany's policies of

the Cold War could not last long. The changes in the international environment, domestic pressure for reform, and, finally, the intensive interrelation between the components of West German foreign policy would not have allowed Bonn to modify its Eastern policy without setting a general revision in motion. To be sure, this process appears to have been initiated inadvertently by the Adenauer and Erhard governments, i.e. without a clear perception of the ultimate consequences (though some individuals in responsible positions were more aware of the implications of their actions than they dared to admit in public at that time). But this should not distract from the impact of the new *Ostpolitik* on the evolution of German foreign policy. After the Western Allies' shift towards a policy of *détente* had eroded the ground on which the structure of Bonn's post-war policy had been erected, the removal of a crucial supporting element was bound to accelerate its collapse.

The domestic debate and the problem of intra-German relations

The foreign policy of the new Democratic Administration in the United States constituted the indispensable context within which the debate in Germany on the German problem gained momentum and crystallized around the discussion of *alternative strategies*. But those strategies, unlike alternative options discussed in the 1940s and 1950s, remained within the limits of the fundamental Western orientation of the Federal Republic and within those set by Kennedy's new policy.

One important early reassessment of policy in Germany, Egon Bahr's proposal of July 1963, for *Wandel durch Annäherung* (change through rapprochement) with East Germany, grew out of a point-by-point examination of the Kennedy programme's relevance to a strategy for dealing with the German division.[98] Bahr concluded that in Germany a policy of all or nothing, free elections or no movement at all, had become meaningless. As in global East–West relations, the interests of the other side—i.e. Russia's interest in not losing East Ger-

---

[98] According to Bahr's own account of the origin of his proposals (in a conversation with the author). Extracts of the proposals are reprinted in Heinrich von Siegler, pp. 311–13.

many—had to be taken into account. But this meant that the idea of overthrowing the GDR was futile, and that German reunification could only occur at the end of a long historical process. Referring to the example of the United States and China, Bahr suggested that regular contacts need not mean official recognition. The two German authorities could co-operate in setting up an intra-German office to identify areas where contacts and co-operation would be mutually useful. The main goal of such activities would be to improve living conditions for East Germans, but change should be gradual, so that revolutionary upheavals would not force the East German authorities or the Russians to resort to repressive action. In fact, the West Germans should consider decreasing their pressure on the East German régime so that the risks involved in granting a relaxation on intra-German contacts would be acceptable to the Communist leadership.

Bahr's analysis was highly unorthodox at that time, and represented the first significantly different proposal from a member of one of the major German political parties since 1960, when the Social Democrats had accepted the European and Atlantic alliance as the basis for West Germany's foreign policy and *Deutschlandpolitik*. Then press secretary and consultant to Mayor Willy Brandt, he was severely criticized by spokesmen of the two governmental parties but some of his ideas enjoyed increasing acceptance and later appeared in a modified form in proposals made by his one-time critics.[99]

The parties themselves, at least officially, adhered for some time to the traditional policy, although under the surface the ferment of change had begun to work. Public opinion was ahead of them until about 1965–6, when the FDP and SPD adopted more unorthodox positions on a number of related issues.

This is not the place to retrace the entire evolution of West German public opinion, but mention should be made of some

[99] For example in the concept of *Änderung durch Einwirkung* (change through gradual influence) and in proposals made (in a speech in Washington in June 1966) by Rainer Barzel, parliamentary leader of the CDU; or the various proposals made by spokesmen of the FDP to handle intra-German contacts through special commissions.

of the earlier contributions. In the early 1960s Peter Bender wrote several important analyses in *Der Monat* and *Die Zeit*, and in 1965 published a book with the programmatic title of *Offensive Entspannung (Offensive Détente)*. His basic thesis was that Bonn must replace policies of hostility and isolation towards the GDR by friendlier and more co-operative attitudes, in order to enable the open-minded elements among the Communist élites to liberalize the East German political system. This thesis, after being shared initially by a minority only and frowned on by the government and parties, gradually became the majority opinion of responsible élites in West Germany. And it can in fact be said that the main, if not the leading, role in examining new ideas was played by newspapers and periodicals. *Die Zeit* and also *Der Spiegel, Süddeutsche Zeitung, Frankfurter Rundschau, Der Monat*, and *Frankfurter Hefte*, to mention but a few, carried on a never-ceasing debate on Bonn's policy. Their analyses, themes, and proposals (including two influential American contributions by Zbigniew Brzezinski and Henry Kissinger)[100] by about 1964–5 began to spill over into a governmental re-examination of Bonn's foreign policy and the official stand of the three major parties.

How far a 'policy of small steps' or 'medium steps' taken to establish relations with the East German authorities should or could go was and still is a hotly debated issue. Johann Gradl summed up the dilemma when he stated that the Germans cannot 'overcome the division of Germany by recognizing it'.[101] But critics suggested that this was convincing only if 'recognition' meant a final renunciation of unity, and not if it implied measures intended to keep the two parts of Germany together. Many critics of past policy favoured dealing with the East German authorities. It should be an important objective of the Federal Republic, they argued, to prevent the rise of two dissimilar and possibly antagonistic German states by maintaining intra-German contacts, which would have as a simultaneous aim the liberalization of East Germany. Even if the position of

[100] Many of them are reprinted or perceptively examined by Theo Sommer in an anthology of writings of that period in Theo Sommer, ed., *Denken an Deutschland* (1966).

[101] Johann B. Gradl, 'Ist Wiedervereinigung aktuell', in Jacobsen and Stenzl, eds., *Deutschland und die Welt* (1964), p. 207.

the régime in East Berlin were thereby strengthened, a hardening of the German division would not necessarily follow. On the contrary, any success in liberalizing East Germany and strengthening intra-German links would improve conditions for the ultimate restoration of some form of German unity.

The advocates of a different policy towards the GDR conceded that a new West German strategy on reunification might indeed solidify the East German régime. It would be difficult if not impossible to achieve the liberalization of the régime against its will, since it could stop or channel into harmless areas any liberalization that undermined its own position. They argued that a West German policy aiming at liberalization in East Germany could not possibly succeed without some co-operation from the ruling élite—not the Ulbrichts, Honneckers, and Fröhlichs, but the second rank of younger, less orthodox, and more flexible party functionaries. They might conceivably come from what Peter Christian Ludz in his important study has called the *Gegenelite* (counter-élite) to the political and ideological leadership, namely the managers and technocrats.[102] The alternative course of hostility and isolation would only strengthen the hard-line Communists, and weaken any potentially progressive group by forcing it to endorse a defensive unity among East German élites.

A policy that aims at East German liberalization through increased intra-German contacts must therefore, according to this school of thought, differentiate between those East German leaders who have presided over the tyranny and suppression of the post-war decades and party functionaries who lean towards a more humane and less dogmatic form of Communism. Through economic concessions and increased official contacts, the Federal Republic could offer the second group prestige and success, in return for improvements in the living conditions of the East German population and measures that preserved or strengthened the relations between the two German societies, e.g. freer movement of persons, ideas, and goods.

The advocates of more contacts with East Germany admitted, however, that to be successful this policy would have to

[102] Peter Christian Ludz, *Parteielite im Wandel* (1967).

resolve one difficult problem: the group of men who had im-plemented Stalinist policies in East Germany still held power and were in a position to prevent the implementation of intra-German contacts. Moreover, it would be difficult for West Germans to draw a line between acceptable and non-accept-able East German partners. After all, it had been the post-war Stalinists (among them Ulbricht himself) who had actively pursued the de-Stalinization of the last few years. It might be possible, however, that a policy which appeals quite openly to the group of less dogmatic party functionaries would find support among the East German leaders, particularly if the Federal Republic made it unequivocally clear that she had no interest in their overthrow.

As has been rightly suggested,[103] the wide variety of views presented in the debate on the Federal Republic's policy on Germany's division was less pronounced on the right than on the liberal centre and left. This is not surprising, since for the former, which had carried the main burden and responsi-bility of past policies, it was more difficult to adopt a critical attitude than for those forces which had been traditionally more critical about it and aloof from its making. Still, the right did not completely abstain from re-examining old poli-cies and advocating change. Many conservative forces sup-ported a more active German *Ostpolitik* though, as we have seen, they were often motivated by a desire to challenge the GDR more effectively. Moreover, some of those politicians and publicists, particularly in the CSU, the Bavarian wing of the CDU, who endorsed de Gaulle's call for a Europe more independent from the United States, and for a reunification of East and West Europe, in their own proposals often deviated from past German positions when it came to issues of the divi-sion. Thus, Franz-Josef Strauss asserted in 1966: 'I do not be-lieve in the possibility of reconstituting a German national state, not even within the frontiers of the four occupation zones, . . . not in the foreseeable future'.[104] As we shall see, he

---

[103] Sommer, *Denken an Deutschland*, p. 7.

[104] *Die Zeit* (German ed.), 8 Apr. 1966. For Strauss's views see in particular his *The Grand Design* (1965) and his June 1966 speech in London, reprinted in *Europa-Archiv*, Aug. 1966.

advocated a solution of the German problem within the framework of European unification.[105]

Though the leaders of both the FDP and the SPD were eager to keep the debate about Bonn's *Deutschlandpolitik* from spilling over into the 1965 election campaign for the Bundestag, the ferment of change became active in both parties. The FDP, while taking part in a coalition government with the CDU, began to press for more low-level contacts with the East German authorities. In March 1965 Erich Mende, then Vice-Chancellor and Minister for All-German Affairs, asserted that unless intra-German contacts were increased, there was a danger that the two parts of Germany would grow further apart; to mitigate this threat he proposed the establishment of two German commissions for intra-German affairs which would act as if they were agents of the four powers.[106]

Among the Social Democrats, the ferment of change was particularly active. Already in 1965, much to the chagrin of the party leadership, which was afraid of the unpredictable consequences for the elections of that year, some groups and *Land* party organizations, notably in Berlin, asked for an abandonment of the past policy towards East Germany and for a more active West German effort to lower East–West tension. But the most important changes in party attitudes took place in 1966 and 1967. Before we examine these more closely we must look at de Gaulle's contribution to the debate in Germany.

A European strategy for the German problem: de Gaulle and the evolution of German policy

De Gaulle's effect on West German thinking and policy transcends the superficially erratic mixture of malaise and euphoria, disagreement and convergence of interests characteristic of Franco-German relations during the Fifth Republic.[107]

---

[105] For another expression of unorthodox views from a CDU politician (which, because of strong criticism, was declared to be a 'private contribution') see the speech of Rainer Barzel in Washington, June 1966, reprinted in *Europa-Archiv*, Aug. 1966.

[106] Address to the 16th Annual Conference of the FDP, 22 Mar. 1965, mimeo. Mende had alluded to a similar proposal in December 1964; see *Bulletin*, 4 Dec. 1964.

[107] On this problem see Alfred Grosser, *French Foreign Policy under de Gaulle* (1967); F. Roy Willis, *France, Germany and the New Europe, 1945–6*, rev. ed., 1968.

His influence is due, first, to the special role France plays in Germany, resulting from France's essential contribution to the reintegration of Germany in the European and Western family of nations and from the deep conviction among the élites of both countries that reconciliation and lasting co-operation between the two nations must be achieved. De Gaulle amplified this inherited influence by the power of his personality and his abilities to maximize France's resources in European politics. He influenced opinion and policy in West Germany by means not only of his views on the context of the German division— the Cold War and the nature of the *status quo*—but even more through his specific strategic proposals for dealing with the German problem in the European context. These proposals came at a crucial moment.

More than any other Western statesman, de Gaulle had stressed the inherently dynamic nature of European politics and, consequently, the transitory character of the Cold War. The East–West conflict was real, but nothing should be done to prevent its transformation into something else. His constant reminders that beneath temporary division into two hostile blocs there was still the old Europe reaching from the Atlantic to the Urals and sharing a common heritage, contrasted with the convictions of West Germans who, as Grosser remarks, tended to regard the East–West conflict as an axiomatic 'given' of world politics.[108] De Gaulle's views were bound to have an effect in West Germany—though initially somewhat under the surface—not only because of France's special role in Germany, but also because Gaullist policy had gained particular credibility with the Germans on the issues of the Cold War: whenever the need arose, he resisted firmly—often more firmly than other Western powers—any Soviet pressure and came to the defence of West German interests (in particular those concerning Berlin).

De Gaulle's reminders that the European division was a dynamic and transitory phenomenon were accompanied by frequent warnings of its danger and reminders that the Germans had a particular responsibility here. When Bonn still

---

[108] Alfred Grosser, 'France and Germany: Divergent Outlooks', *Foreign Affairs*, Oct. 1965, pp. 26–36.

adhered to the tenets of the old 'policy of strength', his advice was:

In the light of the extremely precarious balance that exists between the East and the West, our view on Germany is that it is not opportune, at the present time, to alter the facts as they already exist there. We believe that these facts should be taken as they are and lived with.[109]

Similarly, he was the first Western statesman to recognize the Oder–Neisse line as the final frontier of a reunited Germany and, more important, the first to express clearly what by the mid-1960s had become almost conventional wisdom in the West—namely, that a recognition of the frontiers (and, more unusual, Germany's participation in European integration) was a *precondition* for progress towards German unity.[110]

In addition to defining the changing international context of the German division, de Gaulle suggested a *strategy* for dealing with the issue on a political and diplomatic level. At a press conference in February 1965, he opened his remarks with this incisive statement: 'The German problem is, indeed, *the* European problem'.[111] Offering a detailed analysis of Germany's role in European history, he made it unequivocally clear that Europe must now somehow solve this problem in order to find a lasting equilibrium. The basic idea of the proposed solution was simple: the division of Germany can be overcome only by healing the partition of Europe, and Germany can play a decisive role in this process. Moreover, he showed *sympathy* for the problems of Germany and 'the suffering they entail'—on both points differing from the Americans and British.

---

[109] Press conference, 15 May 1962 (New York, French Embassy, Press and Information Service).

[110] He expressed these views in the context of a firm refutation of Khrushchev's Berlin offensive: 'The reunification of the two parts into a single Germany which would be entirely free seems to us the normal destiny of the German people, *provided* they do not reopen the question of their present frontiers to the west, the east, the north, and the south, and that they move toward integrating themselves one day in a contractual organization of all Europe for cooperation, liberty, and peace'. Press conference, 25 Mar. 1959 (New York, French Embassy, Press and Information Service), my italics.

[111] His emphasis, de Gaulle's press conference of 4 Feb. 1965 (New York, French Embassy, Press and Information Service).

Kennedy's policy (on these issues generally endorsed by the British) was *not* Europe-centred nor couched in terms responding to *German* concerns (except, defensively, in the case of Berlin). Rather, as we have seen, it was global in scope; Germany, like the other allies, was asked to contribute to a relaxation of tensions guided by the two super powers; if returns were possible, then only as a result of the *global détente*. Nor was the Kennedy policy—or, in Britain's case, policy since the 1950s—devoid of a good deal of distrust on the official level.

De Gaulle, in contrast, stressed that priority should be given to the elimination of the 'anomalies' of the German problem, to the suffering and other burdens resulting from the division of the country. The establishment of a somehow unified Germany could only come later. When de Gaulle had made this point in 1959, it attracted no attention.[112] In 1965, however, it coincided with a line that domestic critics in the Federal Republic were putting at the centre of their arguments.

De Gaulle's insistence that the German problem could not be solved 'except by the understanding and combined action of the peoples who have always been, who are and who will remain principally concerned with the fate of the German neighbour—in short, the European peoples' implied acceptance of Germany's frontiers, a settlement with her neighbours of the issue of Germany's armament, etc. All of these points corresponded to ones raised by West German critics of Bonn's policy which, according to them, had failed to take into account the interests of non-Germans.

Similarly, the French President viewed the German problem in a way that critics of Bonn's policy (as well as some supporters of Schröder's *Ostpolitik*) also shared: German policy should be shaken out of its introverted stagnation, produced

---

[112] De Gaulle's formulation of this point in 1959 was made in terms that could have been taken straight out of the government programme of the Great Coalition in December 1966: 'But, pending the time when this ideal [of German unity] can be achieved, we believe that the two separated sections of the German people should be able to multiply the ties and relations between themselves in all practical fields. Transport, communications, economic activities, literature, science, the arts, the goings and comings of people, etc., would be the subject of arrangements which would bring together the Germans within and for the benefit of that which I would call Germanness and which after all is common to them, in spite of differences in regimes and conditions.' Press conference, 25 Mar. 1959, see n. 110.

by Germanocentrism and illusory hopes. The Federal Republic could participate actively in the transformation of Europe and thereby contribute to the solution of her own problems.

Europe, the mother of modern civilization, must establish herself, from the Atlantic to the Urals, in harmony and co-operation, with a view to the development of her vast resources and so as to play, in conjunction with America, her daughter, the role which falls to her in the progress of two billion men who desperately need it. What a role Germany could play in this world ambition of the rejuvenated old continent.[113]

The West Germans reacted strongly to de Gaulle's proposals. Because of his anti-Americanism and the Federal Republic's close relationship with the United States, the debate over de Gaulle's proposals focused initially on one element in his concept—the exclusion of Washington from a European settlement. It was here that public opinion and political leadership in West Germany disagreed with French policy. But de Gaulle's proposals had a greater impact than the initial reactions suggested.

The French President's concepts offered a coherent framework for many of the thoughts that German critics of Bonn's policy had already advanced. Coming from de Gaulle, his pronouncements added respectability to the reformers' views, at least in the eyes of many West German conservatives who were responsive to his views—the same sector of opinion which until then had generally supported an orthodox course on the German problem. In one area, the effect of his supporting the forces of change was more immediately observable: Bonn's new *Ostpolitik*. Not only did de Gaulle's call for peaceful engagement in Eastern Europe find sympathetic ears in West Germany, but the example of his diplomats, touring the Communist capitals, and of Paris, becoming a centre of attraction for East European statesmen, strengthened Foreign Minister Schröder's hand in overcoming resistance within his own party to his reactivated Eastern policy.

That de Gaulle's views came closer to the views of the liberal left than the right in Germany was not immediately recognized by either. The right stressed the benefits of his scheme but

[113] Press Conference, 4 Feb. 1965.

left out some of the sacrifices or changes that it required in German policy. Some wanted to join de Gaulle in creating the larger Europe he envisioned, but passed over in silence such essential aspects of his proposals as the recognition of existing boundaries or the *détente* orientation of his strategy. Thus, Strauss's concept of solving the German problem by removing it from its obsolete nation-state context and by forming an all-European confederation still implied a defeat of Communism.[114]

The German left, in turn, which could not so easily forgive de Gaulle his nationalism with its noticeable impact on Germany, his obstruction of supranational European integration, and his anti-Americanism, at first focused on his threat to West Germany's (and Europe's) co-operation with the United States and to West German security. But after closer examination, these would-be reformers discovered a deeper identity with their own views. Analyses of de Gaulle's policy in the liberal weekly, *Die Zeit*, for example, read differently after 1965. Though they did not share de Gaulle's policy towards the United States, the German liberal left became Gaullist *malgré lui* on the German division.

The crossing of the Rubicon: the beginnings of an intra-German dialogue and the formation of the Great Coalition

By the end of 1965 the debate on Bonn's *Deutschlandpolitik* had reached a critical stage. The government and political parties avoided raising the issues officially, and the election campaign of 1965 did not even touch upon what many voters regarded as Germany's most burning national problems.[115] Many political leaders underestimated the desire for change within Germany at that time, and still believed that public

---

[114] See his *The Grand Design*, and his June 1966 speech. Strauss, while opposing recognition of the Oder–Neisse line at present, sidesteps the issue of the future frontiers by arguing that they play no role in a unified Europe. As one of his advisors put it, the Polish–German frontier would be 'completely irrelevant. Since one can conceive of overcoming the division of Europe only within an all-European federal state, there would simply be no nation-state frontiers any more as soon as the reunited German people has again become the neighbour of the Polish people.' Klaus Bloemer, 'Für eine Weltmacht Europa', in Sommer, ed., *Denken an Deutschland*, p. 182.

[115] Except defensively, when parties and government indignantly rejected the claim of Poland's Chairman of the Council of Ministers, Cyrankiewicz, then on a state visit to Paris, that the Oder–Neisse line was the final western border of Poland.

opinion would not permit them to express publicly the scepticism which many of them held privately about the continued validity of the official West German position. But the pressure for reform from public opinion and from abroad as well as from the internal inconsistencies of Bonn's policy, was bound to generate movement.

The Rubicon was crossed during 1966, when pressure for reform produced significant changes in the policies of the SPD and the FDP, as well as the first concrete measures to implement them. These developments contributed, along with others, to the formation of a new government later that year which adopted a new *Deutschlandpolitik*.

In June 1966 the SPD and the FDP met for their annual conferences. Some of their conclusions were similar, though, of course, the SPD's had more political weight. For the first time, two of the three large parties in West Germany adopted significantly new programmes for a *Deutschlandpolitik*. Led by Brandt, Erler, Helmut Schmidt, and Wehner, the SPD changed its policy on a number of key issues.

The SPD concluded that the Cold War had failed in its offensive objectives and that German reunification was not in the interest of the outside world and would not be so in the foreseeable future. Since the four great powers were deadlocked on these issues, the Federal Republic had to make a greater contribution of her own, in co-operation with her Western allies, in order to use the limited possibilities for progress. To this end she should focus on improving the living conditions of the East Germans and regard an active contribution to the *détente* as the best way to work towards an ultimate solution. To facilitate such a policy the Hallstein Doctrine should be revised *vis-à-vis* Eastern Europe (the first time a major party officially voiced this demand, although in the meantime the government had begun quietly to prepare its revision). The SPD recommended that the Munich Agreement be declared invalid, that a compromise on the Oder–Neisse line be offered, and that nuclear weapons be unequivocally renounced, including participation in multilateral schemes for the Federal Republic—all points on which the West German government should clarify its position in a draft peace treaty.

The SPD recommended pursuing contacts with East Germany on *all* levels; official recognition of the East German government—which the SPD rejected—required intention and could not occur accidentally. The purpose of these contacts would be to ease the burden of the division, to seek better relations on the human level, and to preserve the basic unity of the German nation. The two German régimes should stop threatening each other and coexist peacefully. To overcome the domestic deadlock on these issues caused by competition among political parties, policy should be elaborated in a body representing all parties and the government.[116]

The FDP conference in turn recommended a renunciation of any German participation in schemes for common ownership of nuclear weapons, the creation of all-German technical commissions to discuss intra-German matters under the sponsorship of the great powers, and the establishment of diplomatic relations with East European countries.[117]

A second series of important events in 1966 was initiated by the *East* Germans with the exchange of letters between the Communist Party (SED) and the SPD. Its origin went back to a new evaluation in 1964 by the Soviet and GDR leadership of the state of capitalism and West European politics, particularly of the role of Social Democratic parties. In the autumn and winter of 1965 Ulbricht and Honecker, the two most powerful men in East Berlin, each after a visit to Moscow and obviously following and applying a line laid down by the Soviet leaders, elaborated on the need to form an 'alliance of the working class' in Germany, with the SED and SPD establishing a common front against the 'bourgeois' and 'reactionary' forces in the Federal Republic. The East Germans incessantly invited the SPD in their propaganda to mobilize discontent against the CDU which stagnated under Erhard and to present a genuine alternative to the policy of the 'decaying régime' of Bonn which was beset by crises.[118]

---

[116] *Parteitag der Sozialdemokratische Partei Deutschlands 1966: Protokoll der Verhandlungen* (1966).

[117] See *Süddeutsche Zeitung*, 8 June 1966.

[118] For a detailed analysis of the letter exchange see Gerhard Wettig, 'The SED–SPD Dialogue: Communist Political Strategy', *Orbis*, Summer 1967, pp. 570–81.

The East German initiative was therefore based on the calculation that the situation was ripe for a Popular Front. Trying to exploit a presumed dissatisfaction of the SPD with its leaders (who had allegedly compromised themselves by endorsing the policy of the CDU), Ulbricht, in the name of his party, addressed his first letter of February 1967, not to the SPD party leadership, but to the delegates of the Dortmund party conference and to 'all members and friends of Social Democracy in West Germany', commenting in detail on the SPD's and the Bonn government's foreign and intra-German policies. Ulbricht proposed that the socialist parties in 'the two German states' should seize the initiative and together attempt to overcome the paralysis of movement towards German unity. He suggested that West Germany adopt new policies on arms control and foreign relations and proposed an all-German body composed of representatives of parties and mass organizations in both parts of Germany, to meet alternately in the eastern and western part in order to study concrete measures on the issues of Germany.[119]

The general tone of Ulbricht's letter was fairly conciliatory, though many of his charges had been heard before in the protracted propaganda warfare between the two German régimes. The Social Democratic Presidium, though not the addressee of the letter, replied in March 1967, thus frustrating the SED's attempt to bypass the leadership and to establish direct contact with the party members. The reply rejected many of his accusations and denounced the undemocratic character and inhuman actions of his régime, but left the door open for a continuation of the dialogue. The firm tone of the SPD letter made it easy for other West German parties and the federal government to endorse it, but it was symptomatic of the changed climate in West Germany that a direct exchange of messages between East and West German leaders had become possible. A few years earlier, the mere fact that a letter from Ulbricht had been answered by one of the major parties in the Federal Republic would have led to bitter recriminations—in the improbable event that a party would have dared to reply directly at all.

[119] The letter and the SPD's answer are reprinted in *Europa-Archiv*, Apr. 1966.

This East–West correspondence gained further momentum when, to the surprise of the West German political leaders, the East Germans published the reply of the SPD in full, with all its accusations, in East Berlin's official newspaper *Neues Deutschland*, together with their own proposal to have representatives of the SPD and the East German Communists speak in both parts of Germany.[120] This unprecedented action raised expectations for real progress on the deadlocked issues of Germany. For the first time in its existence the official organ of the Communist Party was in great demand in East Germany.

News reached West Germany that the exchange of letters had stirred up debate and excitement in factory and local cells of the Communist Party and in the East German population at large. The prospect of having the leaders of East Germany come to West Germany to address a rally in Hanover, and of Willy Brandt, Fritz Erler, and Herbert Wehner speaking at a public meeting in Karl-Marx-Stadt (formerly Chemnitz)—both gatherings to be televised over Germany as a whole—fired the imagination of Germans on both sides of the Iron Curtain.

Still, to have Ulbricht or his associates, whom West Germans knew to be the ruthless rulers over seventeen million Germans and the men responsible for the shooting of fleeing Germans, now receive the privilege of addressing a public meeting in the West, was a difficult thing to accept. Opponents of the scheme were in a minority, however, in what became an animated debate on how to handle the exchange. The Bundestag had to pass a special law suspending certain clauses in the penal code so that the East German leaders could enter West Germany without being indicted. Negotiations between the SPD and the East Germans soon reached the stage of arranging the technical details of the meetings—with public discussion in the West occasionally bordering on the comic: the question of whether or not the East German leaders should be greeted with a handshake was a much debated issue.

Then the Communist leaders called off the meetings, using the newly passed special law as a pretext. Two main reasons seemed to have caused this retreat. First, the hope of the SED to drive a wedge between the Social Democratic leadership

120 *Europa-Archiv*, Apr. 1966.

and its rank and file, and to use the party members for an alliance of 'progressive forces' turned out to be illusory. The reaction of the SPD, especially at the Dortmund conference in June, demonstrated not only the firm control of the leaders over the party but also unanimity in the SPD on a pro-Western course based on German membership of NATO and West European institutions. One day after the Dortmund conference had ended, on 7 June 1967, *Pravda* carried an article criticizing the SPD for its anti-Soviet attitude and implying that the hope for a dialogue had failed. The East Germans immediately followed the Moscow line and launched a growing propaganda campaign against the SPD, until it finally called off the planned meetings.

But a second development must have influenced both the East German and Soviet leaders in making this decision. To both, the preparation of a speakers' exchange probably gave enough evidence of growing unrest and rising expectations in the East German population to suggest that the planned gatherings before a national audience could have unpredictable consequences that might possibly slip out of control. Interestingly, the Polish press always stressed the risks for the SED, whereas the Czechs welcomed the planned exchange without reservations.

Though the effort failed, it had several important consequences. In the Federal Republic it broke the spell that had prevented direct dealings with the East German régime. For the first time since the establishment of two German governments, leaders from both sides directly communicated with each other and, equally important, were not criticized for doing so by the public. On the contrary, somewhat to the surprise of the government and the CDU, the SPD mobilized widespread public support. If opinion polls and mass media did not yet provide enough evidence of this endorsement, state elections in North-Rhine Westphalia later in 1966 did; for the SPD scored a striking election victory and there is no doubt that its all-German initiative was one of the causes. What would have been suicidal boldness a few years earlier now paid political dividends. Without the demonstrated changes in the mood of the German electorate in the summer and autumn of 1966, the ensuing evolution of German policy would have been difficult.

Second, the events of those few months in 1966 revealed a feeling of *Zusammengehörigkeit* (belonging together) between the two parts of Germany that the outside world thought (or hoped) was vanishing and that even a number of German politicians were beginning to fear had been lost. Within the Federal Republic this demonstration gave new life to the will to seek new and, if necessary, bold approaches to overcome the division.

Third, the abortive attempt demonstrated the very important point that the Federal Republic need not fear a policy of friendly contacts with the GDR or, indeed, of taking up the very proposals for official relations that the East Germans had been suggesting in the past. On the contrary, direct contacts, far from exposing the Federal Republic to a Communist threat, would represent a challenge to the Communist régime. Obviously, there was a group in the East German leadership willing to enter into a dialogue with the West Germans; perhaps it contained potential allies for the initiatives that many would-be reformers in the Federal Republic had in mind.

Finally, the attempted speakers' exchange also demonstrated the kind of obstacles that any effort for a new policy is bound to meet and has actually met—in both parts of Germany. To the Communist leaders it demonstrated that the all-German issue could awake latent forces in their own society that might take unpredictable turns. To those West German leaders who were sceptical of the new policy, the failure gave some evidence of the futility of making new overtures to East Berlin, which in their opinion only undermined Bonn's earlier position without producing any returns.

In October 1966 it became clear that Chancellor Erhard's reign had come to an end. The general malaise about the stagnating *Deutschlandpolitik* was only one of several reasons for his resignation in November and the formation of a new government on 1 December; other reasons were more important, particularly Erhard's difficulties in providing strong leadership, strains in West Germany's relations with France and the United States, considerable economic and financial difficulties, and a feeble majority in the Bundestag. Given the profound

sense of insecurity characteristic of the German political consciousness it was not surprising that the coincidence of all these
difficulties was perceived by most Germans as a major crisis.
Partly as a result of this perception, the negotiations about a
new coalition took place in an atmosphere of fresh approaches
to many old problems. That also applied to the issues on the
division, and since the SPD had previously committed itself
to a reform of West German *Deutschlandpolitik*, conditions were
favourable for a change of policy.

In a document laying down its position for negotiations on a
coalition government, the SPD called for a new departure
in foreign policy.[121] It demanded, first, that active support of
détente receive priority in West German foreign policy; second,
that relations with the United States and France be mended
and improved and the stagnation of European integration
be overcome; third, that new policies towards Eastern Europe
and the GDR be elaborated, reproducing on this point more
or less the position adopted at the Dortmund party conference.
Most of these demands were reflected in the policy of the
Great Coalition which we shall analyse in the following
chapter.

[121] SPD, *Bestandsaufnahme 1966; Eine Dokumentation* (1966), pp. 19 ff.

7

BONN'S NEW POLICY:
ITS SHAPE, PROBLEMS, AND PROSPECTS

Intra-German relations and the strategy of rapprochement

Two questions have always been particularly important in the Federal Republic's *Deutschlandpolitik*: how can unity be achieved and what should be her relationship with East Germany? We can now sum up the changes of policy on these two issues: Bonn's former policy priority of aiming at institutional reunification in the near future through an East–West agreement, free elections, or overthrow of Communist rule from within, has been abandoned, and along with it the hostile refusal of all contacts with the Communist régime in East Germany. Instead, Germany's main goal is now to improve the living conditions of the East Germans, to reduce the harmful consequences of the division, and to prevent the two parts of Germany from growing further apart. Institutional unity has been relegated to the future after a long historical process has changed the political conditions in Europe.

The new diplomatic objectives of the Great Coalition were expressed in a declaration of policy by Chancellor Kiesinger in February 1967. His pronouncement demonstrates well to what extent the West German position has changed, for two years earlier it would have been unthinkable:

Our advancement of the point of view that there is only one democratically legitimate German state is not intended as tutelage over the people on the other side [East Germany]. We will repeat to them again and again that we want to and shall respect their will. This presupposes that they are allowed to express this will to a growing degree. That this cannot happen overnight and that it is only thinkable as a long evolution, we know that too . . .

Our efforts in what we call the easing of relations [*Entkrampfung*] between us and the other side should be seen in this context. We aim at our countrymen, at the people there. But since there happens to be a political organization on the other side that one encounters in trying to reach the people, we have to seek dispassionately for possibilities to come, through this political organization, into better contact with the people on the other side. We all know that this is a difficult and delicate problem. We do not want to create the impression in the world that we were compromising our legal position [of being the only representative of the German people].[122]

In the same vein, Kiesinger qualified, if he did not abandon, Bonn's former opposition to the East German Communist régime. The idea once held only by 'reformer' critics, that the only way to the people of East Germany was through her rulers, was expressed in the statement just quoted. But he went further and made it clear that the Bonn government accepted the Communist régime as the *effective* ruler of East Germany, though not as the *legitimate* one. Therefore, the Federal Republic declared, she no longer challenged the Communist rule, expecting in exchange that the East German leaders would adopt the same policy towards her. 'We do not want to annex the Soviet Zone, the other part of Germany—I use this expression deliberately since it aims at our countrymen—but we want a reunification in peace and freedom, according to the will of the population of both parts.'[123] Bonn's acceptance of the existing power distribution has been further corroborated by the Great Coalition government's repeated offers to include the GDR in a proposed European system of mutual renunciations of the use of force.[124]

Thus, West Germany's attempt to enter into contact with East Germany has assumed the dynamic orientation which Bonn's earlier critics had advocated: relations between the two parts of Germany as a *means* of liberalizing the Communist régime, of easing the burden of the division, to preserve the heritage of a common nation, and of contributing to a *détente* in Europe through a *détente* within Germany. Whether this policy has scored any successes is, of course, another question to be examined later.

Since the formation of the Great Coalition, Bonn's *Deutschlandpolitik* has gone through a period of unprecedented activity.

---

[122] Speech at Oberhausen, 11 Feb. 1967, in *Bulletin*, 15 Feb. 1967. The same ideas were expressed more cautiously in the government declaration of December 1966, *Bulletin*, 14 Dec. 1966.

[123] Speech at Oberhausen, see n. 122.

[124] Ibid. and Kiesinger's 'State of the Nation' speech of 11 Mar. 1968 before the Bundestag, *Bulletin*, 19 Mar. 1968. For a more recent offer see ibid. 16 July 1968.

Herbert Wehner, one of the chief architects of the SPD's new policy and Minister for All-German Affairs,[125] began to conduct a genuine dialogue through the mass media with East German leaders,[126] and he more explicitly hinted at what the Chancellor had intimated more cautiously in the speech quoted earlier:[127] the possibility of stepping up contacts with the East German régime to an official level if and when it becomes more liberal—especially if an 'Austrian situation' should emerge—implying withdrawal of Soviet troops, neutralization, and evolution towards a more liberal system, or if the régime should evolve along Yugoslav lines.[128]

Then, on 12 April 1967, the SPD Executive Committee and the government addressed two concerted messages to the Communist Party Conference gathered in East Berlin that month.[129] In their letter, the SPD tried to revive the dialogue with the East that had begun with the abortive attempt to arrange a speakers' exchange. Asking the East Germans not to pose 'unacceptable preconditions' for talks, the SPD referred to the message of the Federal government 'to examine what practical things can be done—irrespective of the differences in principle existing between the two parts of Germany—to ease the suffering of the division of our people, and by this to create the conditions for a *détente* within Germany.'[130] (As examples, the government had mentioned improved travel conditions, a border-pass agreement in Berlin, meeting of families, joint development of transport facilities, exchange of electricity, unhindered exchange of publications, etc.)

[125] For a revealing presentation of his views, published shortly before the formation of the Great Coalition, see the collection of interviews in Günter Gaus, *Staatserhaltende Opposition oder hat die SPD kapituliert? Gespräche mit Herbert Wehner* (1966), and the interview in *Der Spiegel*, 24 Oct. 1966.

[126] In particular through his exchange of views with Ulbricht in January and February 1967 on the proposals for intra-German relations which the Communist leader made on New Year's Eve.

[127] See n. 122.

[128] His suggestions were published without his approval by *The Washington Post*, 1 Feb. 1967, but they were not too far removed from views expressed in his television *Deutschlandgespräch*, 9 Feb. 1967. Text published by the SPD in *Tatsachen-Argumente*, no. 222 (Bonn, 1967).

[129] The government's message was simultaneously read by the Chancellor to parliament; text reprinted in *Europa-Archiv*, July 1967.

[130] Ibid.

The Communist authorities replied in the form of a letter from the East German Prime Minister, Willi Stoph. Simultaneously, they stepped up their own demands, agreeing to talks with the West Germans, but only about the establishment 'of normal relations between the two German states', the recognition of existing frontiers, diplomatic relations of other countries with both German governments, etc.[131]

Since this letter was signed by the East German Prime Minister, the question of how to respond to it caused a great deal of debate in Bonn. After some delay, the Federal Republic took yet another unprecedented step, when the *Chancellor* replied directly in June. The gist of his message was that in posing unacceptable preconditions, the East Germans would block any progress towards negotiations. But Kiesinger also suggested that authorized representatives should discuss the concrete measures he had raised in his first letter. At the same time, however (and here again following earlier proposals made by West German critics of Bonn's foreign policy), the Chancellor issued, to parliament and in a diplomatic note to the great powers, a statement that actions undertaken then and in the future to ease the burden of Germany's division—including contacts with the East German authorities—would not signify a change in the government's previous position that a 'recognition of this other part of Germany as a second German state cannot be considered'.[132]

The entire exchange of messages is important for several reasons. Above all, for the first time since the partition of Germany, the two governments communicated directly with each other, and the level of representation Bonn was willing to accept for intra-German contacts has steadily risen. In the 1967 correspondence the Chancellor offered to delegate the Under-Secretary of State at the Chancellery as his personal representative in negotiations. In the 'State of the Nation' message of March 1968 he offered to negotiate personally on intra-German matters with the East German Premier if there was some success in preliminary talks. Of course, it remains to be seen whether the hopes of the 'reformers', that direct dealings between the

[131] Text reprinted in *Europa-Archiv*, July 1967.
[132] Ibid.

two German governments will facilitate the solution of old problems, will come true.

Also, the West German government—again for the first time—acknowledged the existence of a Communist régime (and of the Communist Party) as the *effective* ruler in East Germany, though not as the *legitimate government* of a second German state. Thus Bonn has cast aside a self-imposed restriction that prevented movement, and created some of the preconditions, at least as far as West Germany is concerned, for a more active intra-German policy and the preservation and creation of links between the two German societies.

But the exchange of letters of 1967, like the unsuccessful attempt to arrange a speakers' exchange in 1966, also reveals that the crucial factor determining success or failure in West Germany's friendly overtures towards East Germany lies with the latter—and her Soviet protector.

What does this imply for the future of intra-German contacts? The all-German issue still has a powerful dynamic potential in East German society. If contacts are to mean anything, they will probably cause some reaction among East Germans, and to hard-line Communists opposing such a policy, any reaction, however mild, can always serve as a pretext for their insecure peers and their protectors in Moscow to oppose a 'policy of movement' ostensibly threatening the Communist system. To protect themselves, they have so far resorted to different measures. First, as we have seen, they reversed their previous policy and shunned the contacts they once professed to seek when West Germany was still practising isolation and hostility towards them. Posing preconditions they know to be unacceptable, they hide behind a policy of non-involvement.

East German non-co-operation takes many forms. It is most apparent in the constantly recurring demand for official recognition of the GDR as a prerequisite for negotiations. Ulbricht insisted on this point in his address to the 1967 party conference,[133] and so did Premier Stoph in his letters to Chancellor Kiesinger. Stoph's message also contained a long list of formidable problems to be discussed or settled *before* any of the issues such as improvement of trade or movement of persons could

---

[133] See his speech of 17 Apr. 1967, *Neues Deutschland*, 18 Apr. 1967.

be discussed, *inter alia*: renunciation of the use of force, recognition of all present European frontiers, reduction of military expenditures of the two German states, renunciation of any nuclear role and participation in a nuclear free zone, and support of diplomatic recognition of the two German states by all European states.[134]

The West German government refused to go along with what Kiesinger termed a policy of 'all or nothing' and, instead, insisted on approaching negotiations pragmatically.[135] This may have been the main reason why the Communist leaders carried their demands even further. Stoph's second letter, accompanied by a barrage of hostile propaganda against Bonn,[136] not only reiterated the earlier demands but added the draft for a treaty between the two governments. One article was particularly noteworthy in demonstrating the drastic and unrealistic scope of the East German demands:

The governments of the two German states declare their willingness to enter into negotiations with the aim of finding a peaceful solution to the national question *after* a normalization of their relations, *after* the implementation of a negotiated disarmament and the conclusion of a European security agreement, and *on the condition* that militarism, neo-Nazism, and monopolistic power are overcome.[137]

With the West Germans demanding negotiations on the practical aspects of intra-German relations, and the East Germans insisting on negotiations about the great issues of European and international politics, the two German governments have arrived at a *dialogue des sourds* which suits the East Germans but frustrates the West Germans.

Prolonged failure of Bonn's attempt to initiate an intra-German dialogue undermines the reformist position in West Germany. When reactionary forces among the Communist leaders oppose intra-German contacts, they have some tacit allies in West Germany. By being deliberately unco-operative

---

[134] See his letter of 10 May 1967, cited in n. 131.
[135] See Kiesinger's letter of 13 June 1967, ibid.
[136] See Stoph's address before the East German Parliament on 20 Sept. 1967, *Süddeutsche Zeitung*, 21 Sept. 1967.
[137] See Stoph's letter of 18 Sept. 1967 reprinted in *Europa-Archiv*, Oct. 1967, pp. (D) 476–7, my italics.

and selectively tough—on Berlin, over the Wall, on internal affairs, etc.—die-hard East German Communists have a powerful means of strengthening the position of the orthodox forces in the Federal Republic, who seize on failures or setbacks of reformist efforts either to denounce their futility and danger or to slow down their activities. The West German 'reformers' therefore must overcome resistance on two fronts, and, given the destabilizing consequence of a policy of turning East which we discussed earlier,[138] their task is thus made doubly difficult.

Of course, it is difficult to assess precisely the present impact of West Germany's overtures on the East German leadership, let alone the future prospects of the new policy. But we can say that the action of the West German 'reformers' is not *necessarily* futile, given the absence of East German unanimity on the German issues. The East German leadership is not a monolith but has different groups whose views and interests are not always identical. Decisions are often preceded by struggles, with shifting patterns of majorities. Differences among contending groups may be less pronounced than in a democratic system, but are still significant enough to produce the kind of abrupt policy reversals of which the GDR has seen many in its history.

As long as West German policy towards the GDR was hostile there was enough pressure on the Central Committee and other party bodies to rally unanimously behind the hard line. But with the Federal Republic's friendlier policy, the need for unanimity is less compelling, and different factions may get a chance to assert themselves more freely.[139]

The future evolution of the socialist camp remains, of course, the great unknown when it comes to assessing the prospect of Bonn's strategy towards the GDR. If the camp continues to loosen up and if some of its members, notably Czechoslovakia, can proceed with their liberalization, it heightens both the

---

[138] See above, p. 120–3.

[139] Sudden shifts of majorities and factional differences in the Central Committee can sometimes be deduced from the party organ *Neues Deutschland*. After Kiesinger's first letter to East Berlin a hostile editorial was replaced in the midst of the same edition by a more favourable version. Similarly, prior to Stoph's second letter of September 1967 two leader-writers campaigned in the paper for different policies on the desirability of a continued dialogue with Bonn.

sense of insecurity of the East Germans and their indispens-
ability to the Soviet Union—two powerful catalysts for a
strengthening of orthodoxy and a tightening of party control.
But a further liberalization in the socialist system of states, if
accompanied by a lowering of tensions between East and
West, could lead to a similar process in East Germany. In this
respect the Federal Republic occupies a crucial position.

If West Germany's offers of co-operation are sufficiently
attractive and convincingly abstain from threatening the élites
in East Germany, a majority favouring a rapprochement might
conceivably come into being. The key to the grand solution of
the German problem still lies in Moscow, but the key to some
progress on alleviating the division now also lies in the capitals
of the two German states.

The Federal Republic and the outside world

West Germany's policies towards the GDR and towards the
outside world merge when it comes to Bonn's claim to *Alleinvertretungsanspruch*. West Germany's position here was particularly adamant since it provided the rationale for three
central components of Bonn's foreign policy: (1) the Federal
Republic, with the only freely elected government, alone
represented the whole German nation until such time as
German unity was achieved through free elections and common
institutions; (2) the Communist régime in East Germany could
not be recognized or dealt with on an official level but, on the
contrary, was to be isolated and weakened wherever possible;
and (3) all states recognizing the régime in East Berlin were
committing an unfriendly act towards Bonn. But since these
three policies have now been significantly altered, Bonn's
claim to be the sole representative of Germany has inevitably
weakened. It clashed with, first, Chancellor Kiesinger's new
practice of directly communicating with the East German
Premier and, second, Bonn's acceptance of the Communist
régime as the *effective* ruler of East Germany in order to under-
take concrete steps *in common*, and, finally, with the representation of *two* German governments in a growing number of
East European countries. Solemn statements to the contrary
can perhaps thwart certain undesired political-diplomatic

consequences but they cannot prevent Bonn's new policy from undermining its claim to be the sole representative of the German people.

The evolution of West Germany's priorities with regard to East Germany, Eastern Europe, and the revision of the Hallstein Doctrine have been examined in the preceding paragraphs and in earlier chapters.[140] Suffice it here to add some concluding observations. Once Bonn changed its priorities on reunification and became primarily concerned with the fate of people and contacts between the two societies, it had to deal with the Communist authorities. Indeed, the government of the Great Coalition repeatedly offered to negotiate agreements with East Berlin in a number of fields such as travel conditions, expansion of intra-German trade, unhindered exchange of publications, etc. By implication, Bonn has thereby acknowledged that, at least in the fields it singles out for agreements, the government in East Berlin represents and is responsible for seventeen million Germans, although that form of representation does not comply with the standards of Western democracy.

Bonn's *Alleinvertretungsanspruch* was a constant and real source of irritation to East Berlin and frequently served as a pretext for a hostile response to West German initiatives—as could be observed when Bonn sent its first letter to the East German authorities in the spring of 1967, and when diplomatic relations were established with Rumania. (On both occasions, it will be remembered, the Chancellor demonstratively restated in a declaration before parliament the Federal Republic's claim to be the representative for all of Germany.) To remove this stumbling block for intra-German contacts, Bonn not only began to abandon such official terminology as 'Soviet Occupation Zone', which had affirmed its claim, but some forces in the West German government tried to relegate the whole issue to the background of the controversy by not making the claim as often or as assertively as before. As Herbert Wehner put it: 'Both sides have to disengage themselves somewhat from their respective euphoria and also from their respective claims to be Germany's only legal representative.'[141]

---

[140] See above, pp. 9–11, 20–23, 34–49, 74 ff.
[141] In a report to the SPD, *Die Welt*, 6 July 1967.

Paradoxically, every success of Bonn's new policy of intra-German contacts further undermines its claim to represent all Germans by expanding the area of co-operative undertakings where the Federal Republic accepts the government of East Germany as a partner and an agent for the Germans living there. But then, this erosion of Bonn's *Alleinvertretungsanspruch* is not necessarily irreconcilable with West Germany's interests. To many responsible West Germans, including members of the present cabinet, it is an inevitable by-product of a far-sighted policy of contacts with East Germany. If, with Western help, a relatively free and liberal political system emerges in East Germany, few West Germans would deny the government in East Berlin the right to speak in the name of the East German population. As Foreign Minister Brandt has put it, 'the more freedom the régime in East Berlin grants its people, the more acknowledgement and approval it will find in the world'.[142] The majority opinion among the élites of the Federal Republic now seems to evolve towards the view: rather have all Germans free and in two states than perpetuate the absence of freedom for a large number of them by acting in the futile hope of early reunification in one state.

Bonn's new *Ostpolitik* has the same effect, only more conspicuously. Despite solemn legal reservations, restating the *Allenvertretungsanspruch* (attached to the Federal Republic's new initiatives and the opening of diplomatic relations with Rumania) *two* German governments are now accredited in three European socialist countries (and have representation on a 'lower' level in all the others except Albania), and each speaks effectively for its territory and population. Moreover, the East European governments have denied Bonn the right to speak for the East Germans. The growing engagement of West Germany in the Communist countries led to an intensive diplomatic counter-offensive conducted by East Berlin with the support of Moscow, resulting in a series of pledges of mutual support and assistance treaties.[143]

---

[142] 'Entspannungspolitik mit langem Atem', *Aussenpolitik*, Aug. 1967 (also published in *Bulletin*, 11 Aug. 1967).

[143] For a chronology and a useful collection of documents, see *Europa-Archiv*, Mar. and Apr. 1967.

E

It is true that Rumania did not meet the East German demand, strongly supported by the Soviet Union and Poland,
that no socialist country have diplomatic relations with Bonn
unless the Federal Republic recognizes East Germany, accepts
the existing borders, and renounces any nuclear role. But both
governments agreed to disagree in public on the question of
which German government could speak in the name of which
population. It was during negotiations with Rumania on the
occasion of Brandt's first visit to Bucharest in August 1967
that the Foreign Minister took a major step away from the
Alleinvertretungsanspruch. Referring to the Rumanian position,
he declared:

We also agree that, with regard to the problems of European
security, the existing relations have to be accepted as a point of
departure, and all states regardless of their size have to fulfil equally
important tasks in creating a European peace order. *That also applies
to the two political systems [politische Ordnungen] which at present exist on
German soil.*[144]

In modifying its policy on the occasion of establishing diplomatic relations with Rumania, Bonn, of course, also gave the
Rumanians a reward as well as an argument for defying the
pressure from Moscow and East Berlin. Bucharest could coun-
ter charges of neglect of socialist interests by pointing out that
it had helped to induce Bonn to take a different attitude.

Bonn's most important revision to its claim to be the sole
legitimate representative of all of Germany was its re-establishment of diplomatic relations with Yugoslavia in January 1968.
Yugoslavia had always been a special case since, in pursuance
of the Hallstein Doctrine, Bonn broke off relations with Yugoslavia when Belgrade recognized the GDR in 1957. But when the
reactivated *Ostpolitik* resulted in a revision of the Hallstein
Doctrine, Yugoslavia could initially not be fitted into the legal
and political logic of that revision. While it could be argued
that the East European countries had no choice but to recognize the GDR when they were established as Communist
states (in Germany this is known as the 'birthmark theory'),
Belgrade recognized East Germany only in 1957 and then of

---

[144] Speech of 3 Aug. 1967, *Süddeutsche Zeitung*, 5 Aug. 1967, my italics.

its own free will. Many German leaders were afraid that with the re-establishment of diplomatic relations with Belgrade, the Hallstein Doctrine would lose its sting, and that a host of other countries would then feel free to recognize East Germany. But *Realpolitik* as much as economic interests made it advisable for the German leaders to reopen relations with a country which was influential in the socialist as well as in the Third World, and which represented their most important commercial partner in Central and South East Europe.

Both governments had been quietly working towards a settlement for some time, but only after protracted political probing all over the globe, including a visit by Chancellor Kiesinger to Asia, was Bonn sufficiently sure that the establishment of diplomatic relations with Belgrade would not lead to a chain reaction of recognitions of East Germany by other countries. With this obstacle removed, the Federal Republic and Yugoslavia established relations in January 1968.

Bonn's new Eastern policy not only eroded the *Alleinvertretungsanspruch*, but also gave the fatal blow to a once-central element of Bonn's policy—namely, that reunification was the prerequisite for *détente*. After the formation of the Great Coalition, the old priorities were reversed: a *détente* became the means of achieving a solution of the German problem. 'We know that the German questions can be solved only as part of a peaceful solution (*Friedensregelung*) for all Europe and that this can only be furthered by a state of mutual accommodation between East and West. We do not make our policy of *détente* dependent on progress in regard to the German problem.'[145] This approach implies the abandonment of West Germany's postwar diplomatic encapsulation *vis-à-vis* the East, and her re-emergence as an international actor in Eastern Europe. We have analysed above the dangers which may arise from such an involvement both for Germany and the West, but a further consequence should be stressed: a policy that seeks a solution of the German problem in the context of a general *détente* calls for an *active* German contribution to a relaxation of tension. West German policy has rediscovered the need to contribute actively to the processes of change on a

[145] Brandt, 'Entspannungspolitik mit langem Atem'.

vaster international plane. Few political leaders in Germany talk of the German problem without referring to the need to create a new 'European peace order',[146] or to overhaul fundamentally the alliances.[147] Others mention a final German renunciation of a nuclear role as a contribution to a new European system.[148] The SPD tends to advocate more change than the CDU, but there is a growing consensus among all the main political forces in West Germany that cautious movement towards a new European system is desirable. For a country that tended to be horrified by any change in the international environment except in the form of a collapse of the Communist system, this is no minor evolution.

The Berlin problem

An analysis of the main issues and prospects of West Germany's new policy would be incomplete without examining the Berlin problem. Of all the issues connected with the division of Germany, this is particularly complex and fraught with uncertainties. As we have seen, Berlin played a significant role in the evolution of Bonn's policy.[149] The building of the Berlin Wall in 1961 and later the pass agreement with the East German authorities added momentum to the re-examination of old policies and the consideration of new strategies. But Berlin was also the place where, in connexion with the pass agreement, concrete political steps were undertaken which deviated from the Federal Government's policy of that day and which, it turns out, foreshadowed policies of the Great Coalition.

The Great Coalition's belief that it was unrealistic to expect radical change in the international system (including early reunification), and that Germany should pragmatically seek gradual change, had already been stressed in Berlin and followed in connexion with the pass agreement. Its policy of giving priority to humanitarian concerns and easing the consequences

---

[146] See, e.g., Chancellor Kiesinger's speech at Oberhausen on 11 Feb. 1967.

[147] See, e.g., Willy Brandt, 'Entspannungspolitik mit langem Atem'.

[148] See Helmut Schmidt, *Tatsachen-Argumente*, no. 205 (1966). This policy has also been part of the FDP's official platform since their party conference in 1966. For a restatement of their views see the *Bundestag* debate of October 1967, *Süddeutsche Zeitung*, 14 Oct. 1967.

[149] See above, pp. 80–85, 90–91.

of the division, even if it meant dealing with the Communist authorities, had also been practised in Berlin, when the West Berlin city administration negotiated an agreement with the GDR to liberalize temporarily the ban against movement of persons in the divided city. This is not to say that the Great Coalition ratified or simply fell into line with policies first worked out in Berlin, but only that there is a connexion between the two (which is underlined by the fact that, along with Mayor Willy Brandt, who became Vice-Chancellor and Foreign Minister, other architects of earlier Berlin policies moved to high posts in Bonn).[150]

Though some of the disputes and policy differences that existed between the West Berlin city administration and the government in Bonn disappeared with the formation of the Great Coalition, Berlin's status remains as precarious as ever. West Berlin's specific contribution to West Germany's function as link and barrier in the international system has not changed. Due to its simultaneous vulnerability and political importance, West Berlin remains the advance outpost of the West and the area where the balance between the two opposing systems can most easily be upset. At the same time, this Western island reinforces the domestic dimension between East and West Germany, and interlocks the two polities. This has been vividly demonstrated again by the student unrest in West Berlin and reactions to it in East and West Germany. The 'escalator syndrome' is constantly in effect in Berlin where disputes immediately affect relations between the opposing alliances—often at the highest level—and so is the 'externalization syndrome', since here 'domestic' issues often become international ones from the start or very shortly after.

The various suggestions in the West for changing Berlin's status—such as neutralization or internationalization—do not appear to resolve the precariousness of Berlin's situation or its potentiality as a source for disruption. Nor, for more obvious reasons, do Communist proposals to transform Berlin into a

---

[150] Klaus Schütz, Senator (i.e. Minister) in the Berlin government became Under-Secretary in the Foreign Ministry until his return to Berlin in October 1967 to become the new Mayor, and Egon Bahr, Brandt's press secretary, joined the Foreign Ministry as Head of Policy Planning.

'free city' or to make it a third German state, for they implicitly destroy or weaken one of the essential elements in the present equation, that of Western security guarantees, while leaving intact others that are at the root of its position as a potential source of instability, notably its vulnerability and its political importance to the West Germans.

For a number of years Bonn has been under strong and concerted pressure from Communist governments to make concessions to the 'three-state theory'. Ingenious formulas were developed by Bonn to extend to West Berlin the application of trade, cultural, and other agreements between the Federal Republic and the socialist countries,[151] but the net effect has been a weakening, at least in official documents with East European countries, of West Germany's assertion that she acted on behalf of West Berlin as a (special) part of the Federal Republic. The Great Coalition's agreement of the summer of 1967 to establish consular relations with Czechoslovakia no longer contained the customary 'Berlin clause'; instead, the two parties settled the matter in a secret exchange of letters. But then, even a weak 'Berlin clause' would have offended East Berlin which had put heavy pressure on Prague to use the negotiations for getting official West German acknowledgement of the 'three-state theory'. Not only Bonn made concessions to Eastern demands; in West Berlin the city administration negotiated the 1963 pass agreement with the GDR authorities on its own, albeit formally not as a 'third German state'.

Under the Great Coalition, the attempt to find a 'new role' for Berlin that would help alleviate the problems of the divided city has continued among the political leaders of West Berlin. After the departure of Willy Brandt to Bonn, the idea of a small degree of disengagement from the Federal Republic has had some support in the Berlin SPD, including some members of the city government. To the embarrassment of the West Berlin city administration, which later disavowed him, the Senator for Economic Affairs, at a fair in Moscow in August 1967 not only conferred with the Soviet Minister for Foreign

---

[151] For several years such agreements had a 'Berlin clause' stipulating that they applied where the Deutsche Mark (West) was legal currency, thus including West Berlin.

Trade, but also hinted at the future possibility of separate trade agreements between Moscow and West Berlin.[152] Shortly thereafter a special meeting of the Berlin SPD unanimously passed for adoption by the party the recommendation that allied guarantees and integration with West Germany should remain the basis for West Berlin's security and survival, but that the 'particular margin of manoeuvre' offered by Berlin's position under direct Allied responsibility should be used to make a special contribution to intra-German relations through direct negotiations with the government in East Berlin.[153]

To many West Berliners, the idea of transforming the city from a Western outpost into a bridge between East and West has great appeal. If it requires some differentiation between Berlin and the Federal Republic on certain matters, this is understood, not as a step towards a 'third German state', but as a prerequisite and means to act as a dynamic force of East–West rapprochement. Of course, such a course poses difficult problems for Bonn as well as for the whole West, for if all that happens is that Berlin's links with the West are weakened without obtaining the expected results, such a policy may well end up exposing West Berlin even more to Eastern pressures.

Discord over policies

Our repeated references to the differences in outlook between political groups on the issues of divided Germany raise the problem of the domestic implications of the new *Deutschlandpolitik*. How do the new policies affect stability in the Federal Republic, and how do domestic West German politics influence its prospects for success?

Since the evolution of the international environment and Bonn's new policies on the division of Germany are inextricably interconnected, instability can have external or internal causes, or both. As we have seen, the 'external' causes include isolation of the Federal Republic in the West, decline of European and Atlantic frameworks of co-operation, protracted hostility towards West German initiatives, or disturbance from the outside of what we have called the 'balance of gains and sacrifices.' In most cases, external disturbance is likely to be amplified by

[152] See *Die Welt*, 1 Sept. 1967.   [153] Ibid. 25 Sept. 1967.

internal strains. Domestic support for the policies originating in the Cold War—the 'policy of strength', isolation and non-recognition of the GDR, *Alleinvertretungsanspruch*, or non-recognition of the borders—is still sufficiently strong to clash with the new policies.

Moreover, since the new policies emphasize results—patience being one of the weaker ingredients of German political culture—they are vulnerable on two counts: on many issues their costs are concrete and visible, whereas their returns remain in the realm of promise and visions. Supporters of the old policies object on the grounds of their excessive costs, and argue for a stop or slow-down, while proponents of the new policies blame West Germany's insufficient conversion to the new course for any failure, and consequently press for further advances. The policy of intra-German contacts, the first group argues, has upgraded the GDR and pushed the Federal Republic towards recognition of East Berlin: but where are the signs of improvement in intra-German relations, let alone the liberalization of the Communist régime, that this policy aims for? On the contrary, argues the second group, as long as the GDR is not accepted and recognized, progress on these objectives is unlikely. The debate has followed a similar pattern on other issues.

Since autumn 1967 disagreements on the new policies have begun to strain both domestic politics and the Great Coalition. On the issues of recognizing the GDR and the Oder–Neisse line, attacks from groups wanting either a more cautious policy or a more daring one had grown sufficiently strong for the government to find it necessary to defend itself against both. Chancellor Kiesinger attacked the latter as an *Anerkennungspartei* (recognition party) which, impatiently seeking panaceas, was trying to guide the Federal Republic on to a dangerous course.[154] To protect itself in turn against the growing and potentially more powerful criticism from the first group of sceptics, the government saw fit to state simultaneously that recognition of the GDR or the Oder–Neisse line was out of the

[154] See Kiesinger's contribution to the *Bundestag* debate of October 1967, *Süddeutsche Zeitung*, 14 Oct. 1967.

[155] See the *Bundestag* debate of October 1967, ibid., and the statement by a government spokesman on the Oder–Neisse line, *Süddeutsche Zeitung*, 17 Oct. 1967.

question.[155] A number of government members launched a campaign on the gains of the new policies in the form of a new and more peaceful image of West Germany to the outside world and stressing the long-term nature of their policies.

Disagreements on the new policies used to cut across party lines, though from the start of the Great Coalition the critics of the new policies were more frequent among the Christian Democrats. The differences between the two coalition partners have become more marked, and may well deepen in the future. The 1968 party conference of the SPD exposed some of these disagreements when the Social Democrats recommended 'to respect and recognize', until a final peace settlement, the present European borders, and their coalition partner rejected their proposal.[156] There had earlier already been numerous tensions within the Coalition, and the pattern had always been the same: the conservative forces of the CDU, notably the CSU (occasionally reinforced by some individual SPD deputies close to refugee organizations) opposing the SPD and parts of the CDU in their attempts to modify old policies. In February 1968 Foreign Minister Brandt, faced with strong criticism from within the CDU and the CSU, even threatened to resign.[157]

The Great Coalition embraces two different, if not contradictory, conceptions of a future solution to the German problem. To the first, Bismarck's *kleindeutsche Lösung* of a unitarian German state, a *Reich*, remains a relevant model to guide German policy. Its support is diffuse, but there are identifiable pockets of strength among conservative Protestants, older civil servants (notably diplomats), refugees, and the extreme right. The second conception – partly as a reaction against the first – is groping for a different solution of the German problem, if necessary in the form of a radical departure from concepts of past decades and of former German régimes. Its contours remain somewhat indistinct, but the common factor is a willingness to accept a political organization of Germany based on separate political entities, linked with each other and neighbouring entities in various forms of association, co-operation, confederation, etc. Its supporters can be found particularly

[156] See above, p. 49.   [157] *Die Welt*, 12 Feb. 1968.

F

among Catholics, Protestants left of centre, and more frequently in the younger generation than in the older.

The impossibility of immediate unification in one state makes the new *Deutschland* – and *Ostpolitik* – acceptable to the 'Neo-Bismarckians' and imperative to the reform-minded 'associationists'. The truce between them is made possible by implementing a policy based on association between two German states for the *near* future, while proclaiming a unitarian German state as its eventual goal for the *distant* future.

The outstanding advantage of this formula is that it facilitates the development, assessment, and testing of new policies on Germany's crucial issues with the consent or co-operation of different and normally opposing groups in German politics. Its weakness is that to the 'Neo-Bismarckians' success of 'associationist' policies tends to preclude their own solution whereas failure reconfirms it, but in either case the truce is undermined. The unresolved tensions between these two concepts are therefore more likely to come to the surface not only in coalition politics but in German political life in the period ahead.

Another legacy of the past burdens the Great Coalition, as, indeed, it would have burdened any German government in the 1960s. This is the inherent contradiction, alluded to earlier, between the Western policy of integration and the 'national' rhetoric of reunification which Adenauer pursued for a decade. As Arnulf Baring rightly observed, 'considerateness for all-German sentiments made him pursue the problematical attempt to justify his Western policy as the true *Ostpolitik*', thus undermining his own Western concepts and achievements.[158] These unresolved questions are now coming to the forefront again, creating conflicts in the German body politic and inevitably straining a coalition government which encompasses fundamentally different political groups.

Apart from the legacies of the past and reformers' perpetual dilemma of displeasing either the sceptics or the radicals or both, the mechanics of decision-making in the Great Coalition are only partially able to regulate conflict. Decisions on *Deutschlandpolitik* are supposed to be made by a special cabinet com-

---

[158] 'Die westdeutsche Aussenpolitik in der Ära Adenauer', *Politische Vierteljahresschrift*, ix/1 (1968), p. 47.

mittee consisting of the Chancellor, the Foreign Minister, and the Minister of All-German Affairs, occasionally reinforced by a minister whose field of activities is affected by the deliberations. These discussions, mostly conducted without aides, are informal in style and often leave major issues unresolved. They do not result in detailed written instructions which can guide policy on all levels of administration. When cabinet members sometimes differ in their public statements they may perhaps violate the spirit of an agreement but rarely the letter, which is usually non-existent.

Disagreements within the Great Coalition have so far slowed down the new *Deutschlandpolitik*, but they have not paralysed it. Compromise was usually possible because supporters of the new policies were in the majority. In fact, at the time of writing, this majority would exist in any other coalition, since the third party, the FDP, is even more committed to change than the CDU or the SPD. A continuation of the new course would only be threatened if a hostile majority would form against it in the West German body politic. But that is something one can only speculate about, since a multitude of other uncertain factors would determine such an outcome, above all the evolution of the international situation and the success of the new policies; their protracted failure could, indeed, erode the present domestic support.

But even if Bonn's new *Deutschlandpolitik* were to face a hostile majority at home, are there alternatives to the present course? Could the Federal Republic return to a policy of hostility and isolation *vis-à-vis* East Germany after she has moved a long way towards recognizing the GDR *de facto* as a second German state with which she wants to establish a working relationship? Could Bonn freeze or reverse its active diplomacy towards Eastern Europe after it has revised central tenets of its post-war foreign policy such as the Hallstein Doctrine and the *Alleinvertretungsanspruch* in order to open the door to Eastern Europe? Could West Germany abandon her policy of supporting a *détente* and become a lone bastion of anti-Communism in the West?

For the time being, possibilities for a change of the present policy no doubt exist, but viable alternatives to the basic options of the present course do not seem to be in sight, not even in the form of a revival or creation of Western schemes, Atlantic or West European. Contrary to some opinions,[159] Western frameworks for co-operation do not represent an alternative to Bonn's new *Deutschlandpolitik*, as long as the two are generally regarded as compatible in the West and as long as Bonn's new course is identical with or endorsed by Western policies. But given the inevitable internal tensions in the wake of the new policy on the division, this means that the Federal Republic is condemned to a protracted period of strains in domestic politics and in coalition governments.

[159] For example an otherwise perceptive Scandinavian study of the German problem: Martin Saeter, *Okkupation, Integration, Gleichberechtigung* (1967), pp. 85 ff.

8

CONCLUSION

The interaction of domestic and international politics: the impact of change

FOR slightly more than a decade the Federal Republic has occupied a special role in the international system of bipolarity. We can now sum up what specific structures of interaction exist between German and international politics, and how they have been affected by the changes of the last years.

The context of Germany's foreign policy of the 1950s was characterized by three essential features: the environmental origins of this foreign policy; West Germany's place in the structure of the international system and the ensuing patterns of interaction between German and international politics; and finally, the balance between gains and sacrifices, stability and instability.

The environmental origins of West Germany's domestic and foreign policies have been clearly marked. We went so far as to suggest that the Federal Republic was not a régime that created a foreign policy but a foreign policy that created a régime. Both German political systems were products of the bipolar system of the East–West struggle. Not only their foreign policies with their respective integration in East or West, but also their internal constitutional and political organization were heavily determined by the international environment. Bonn's foreign policy became an integrated part of the 'policy of strength' whose objectives were identical with regard to East Germany and Eastern Europe: the collapse of Communist rule.

The changes of this environment are well known. Though a basic East–West antagonism still exists, the *détente* has transformed the once exclusively hostile bipolar system into what has been called 'muted' or 'co-operative' bipolarity.[160] Moreover, some of the Western organizations for co-operation in the West, including European integration, in which the Federal

---

[160] The first term was introduced by Hoffmann, *Gulliver's Troubles*, the second by Carl Friedrich Freiherr von Weizsäcker, 'Über weltpolitische Prognosen', *Europa-Archiv*, Jan. 1966.

Republic evolved, are going through a critical phase of reassessment and adaptation.

But considering the Federal Republic's deep sense of insecurity and the scope of these changes, she has *so far* adapted to them with surprising ease. One has to consider how radically she has modified her policies: she no longer stakes everything on German reunification in the near future. She has shelved the Hallstein Doctrine, relaxed her stand on the borders, and has fallen into line with the Western policy of *détente*; hence her attempt at peaceful involvement in Eastern Europe. In domestic and foreign policies she is trying to come to terms with the German division and the existence of the Communist régime in East Germany, which she attempts to induce to a policy of intra-German contacts. In domestic politics, the climate of hostility towards the Communist régime has subsided and may at some future point spill over into the field of political organization and constitution (for example, in the form of a repeal of prohibitive legislation against the Communist Party).[161]

Second, Germany has occupied a unique position in the international system of bipolarity. It is on her soil that the two hostile systems meet and face each other with a high concentration of military power in the two German régimes as their respective outposts. It is here that the scales of the international balance can most easily be tipped. But the two German régimes still form part of one German nation and consequently a *domestic* context with its characteristic behaviour patterns. Paradoxically, within Germany the two antagonistic systems at once stand off from and penetrate each other. The consequence has been that in divided Germany two syndromes are simultaneously at work: external problems affecting Germany tend to be 'escalated' because they can have immediate far-reaching consequences in the international system as a whole as a result of both the intra-German dynamics and Germany's international position; internal problems within either German régime tend to be 'externalized' because they almost automatically become questions of international importance, be it the rise of a right-wing party in West Germany or a temporary

---

[161] Such a proposal has been made by various personalities, e.g. Willy Brandt; see *Die Welt*, 11 Nov. 1967.

majority favouring a dialogue with Bonn in East Germany.

Berlin accentuates this pattern of interaction between domestic and international politics. As a vulnerable Western outpost surrounded by Communist territory, West Berlin has been a major arena of the East–West confrontation, and a trip-wire for international stability. But, at the same time, because of its location and its political importance to the West Germans, Berlin has also intensified the 'domestic' dimension in intra-German relations, interlinking the two German régimes and rendering complete disengagement, if it were desired, practically impossible, except as a result of Berlin's absorption into the GDR which the West cannot accept. Indeed, the decision of the World War II Allies to divide among themselves the city *within* Russian-held territory, for all the constant international headache it created, in retrospect appears as a momentous decision to preserve a single German nation, since it made complete separation of the two German régimes impossible.

Changes in the international environment and within Germany have not affected this or the ensuing patterns of interaction between domestic and international politics. Though the intensity and the content of the East–West conflict have changed, the antagonism is still there, and European stability can still be upset in Germany, though perhaps less easily with both sides having become more cautious. West Berlin's vulnerability is as great as ever, and though West Germany has become more secure and less hostile towards East Germany, the latter is insecure enough to feel obliged to hide behind her own policy of isolation and hostility. The 'escalating' mechanism continues to work, as was demonstrated by the Soviet intervention in 1966 to block a speakers' exchange between East and West Germany. And the 'externalization' mechanism still works, as the sensitive Western reactions to domestic developments in the Federal Republic constantly show.

Lastly, the international environment of the post-war period provided a balance of gains and sacrifices to West Germany that partly explains the domestic stability the Federal Republic enjoyed since her establishment. In exchange for her temporary acceptance of the division of Germany and her active contribution to the anti-Communist struggle, the Federal

Republic was granted a number of gains, such as readmission into the Western family of nations, aid for reconstruction, recognition as the sole legitimate representative of the German people, support for her reunification efforts, endorsement of the West German position on the borders, and so on.

This balance of gains and sacrifices was radically changed by developments in the last years. Many gains in the form of support for Bonn's *Deutschlandpolitik* were either weakened or withdrawn, whereas the sacrifices remain: the division of Germany seems to be here for a long time to come. The Federal Republic's new policies on the division can be viewed as an attempt to cope with this challenge and to create a balance of gains and sacrifices on a different plane, with different constituents.

Partially deprived of the support that came from the outside during her formative years, trying to redefine her purpose in the face of dim hopes for unity, with an internal balance to be recreated and the inevitable domestic strain of the new policies to be absorbed, the Federal Republic is now going through the most severe and crucial test since her establishment. The Great Coalition of 1967 is no mere accident, but grew out of the justifiable desire to establish a broad political basis for coping with a series of difficult problems considered by most Germans as reflecting a deeper crisis of the young Republic. However, the Coalition, while creating better conditions for dealing with these problems, has also engendered serious strain on the domestic structure. With conflict between the major parties of the right and left being contained within the Coalition, forces of opposition have been encouraged to pursue their goals outside the framework of parliament and established democratic parties, and thereby to challenge the democratic consensus of the Federal Republic.

Two states in one German nation?

Recent developments raise a more fundamental question as old as the modern European nation-state and at the root of Germany's past search for identity: what should the political entity be within which the German-speaking people are to organize themselves in European and world politics? It is a question of prime importance to Europe as well, since the political organization of the Germans, more numerous than any other European people except the Slavs, and living within ill-defined borders, has profoundly affected European stability.

The Germans achieved their common state (which excluded the Austrians) only in 1871, and with Germany's East–West division occurring in the aftermath of World War II, three quarters of a century of a unified German state came to an end. But the record of a united Germany has not been encouraging. Responsibility for two world wars, inability to establish a stable democracy, Auschwitz and all it represents, are associated with this period of German history. A causal relationship between this record and a unified German state is by no means entirely proven, but to many Europeans and Germans the question has arisen whether a united Germany is desirable, or—to use the dichotomy of Germany as a *Staatsnation* and *Kulturnation* which has played a great role in German thinking since the nineteenth century—*should* Germany as a *Staatsnation* be recreated?

The question is not new. Germany has existed as a *Kulturnation*—and a flourishing one, too—for a long time. For a minority of the late eighteenth and the nineteenth-century German thinkers, with Schiller and Goethe as their most eminent representatives, a unified state had a lower priority than Germany's spiritual growth and the creation of a better society. After World War II, to many Germans a united German state, as well as the European nation-state as such, appeared discredited by the events of the past. To them, European unification was the obvious solution which would sooner or later make the nation-state in Europe dispensable. To other Germans the problem was a moral one. To them the Germans had gambled away the right to be unified.[162] Though the latter group is in a minority in contemporary West Germany, questions about the desirability of and conditions for a unified German state are in the minds of many political and intellectual leaders in Germany who are concerned about the future of German policy. For the liberal faction, the West German claim to speak for all of Germany and her readiness for reunification, as K. D. Bracher put it, 'depend

---

[162] A prominent example is Karl Jaspers; see his *Lebensfragen der deutschen Politik*.

entirely on whether West Germany's democracy proves itself as a social and spiritual way of life and not just as a formal constitutional construction', in other words, whether the Federal Republic is able, for example, to practise effectively a genuinely free and social democracy, to contain excessive economic power and reactionary tendencies, to protect personal liberties, and to overcome blind obedience to authority.[163]

The very inflexibility of the *status quo* in Germany and the need psychologically to absorb the certainty of continued division in the next decades may in fact give a new impetus to the historical question about the future of a German *Staatsnation*. For the time being, however, German thinking and policy are focusing on the more immediate problem of adapting politically to the prospect of a long period of partition. There are indeed a number of conditions and forces that keep alive or work towards some form of German unity. Four sets of factors can be distinguished. Within West Germany, German unity continues to be given top priority by all political parties and is endorsed by the public at large, though few Germans believe that it can be brought about in the near future. Unity therefore promises to remain a main objective of West German policy.

East German attitudes are, of course, difficult to ascertain, and opposition to unity is manifest among the Communist leadership. Through legal measures and a major propaganda campaign, it declared the end of a single German citizenship, science, language, and culture.[164] The explanation for this puzzling reversal of what used to be a socialist version of all-German nationalism partially lies in the changes in Bonn's policy, since otherwise East Germans could press their leaders to respond favourably to Bonn's friendly overtures and pleas for contacts in the name and for the sake of a common Germany. To claim the existence of two German states no longer provides enough shelter. The East Germans' attack on those elements which the German nation has in common, appears to aim at a

---

[163] Karl Dietrich Bracher, *Deutschland zwischen Demokratie und Diktatur* (1964), p. 136.

[164] The campaign was launched at the beginning of 1967 though it reverted to earlier arguments about the inherent difference between socialist and capitalist science, language, theatre, etc. The text of the law of February 1967 establishing a separate GDR citizenship is reprinted in *Europa-Archiv*, Mar. 1967.

remaining source of unrest and potential generator of change in Germany, and indicates their apprehension about the latent dynamics of intra-German contacts.

But then, East German policy on Germany as a nation, like many other Communist policies on German issues, has been ambiguous and contradictory. To abandon the idea of a common nation also deprives the East German Communists of a powerful means of challenging the West German régime. They had once argued that only in the 'Peasant and Worker State' had the visions of socialism's founding fathers (Germans after all) come true; therefore the GDR alone represented the 'true and better Germany', called on by history to complete the revolution in the other part of the country, and not to falter in her efforts until socialism reigned throughout the entire nation.[165]

The East German Communists are therefore caught in a dilemma: on the one hand the decline of even the concept of Germany as a single nation would provide better protection from the intra-German dynamics and the ever-present West German challenge to the Communist régime in the East; on the other hand, to strike at the idea of the German nation is tantamount to retreating from the old ambition of extending socialist influence, if not rule, to all of Germany.

Should the East German leaders abandon the objective of eventual reunification, their basis for challenging the Federal Republic would be no different from, and as weak as, the basis for challenging the political régimes of, say, France or Britain. The concept of a German nation and of eventual German unity is therefore as important to the East German régime as it is to the Federal Republic.

For these reasons it is not surprising that the East German leaders have pursued contradictory policies simultaneously. In the same year that East Berlin launched its campaign against the concept of a common German citizenship, culture, science, etc., and renamed the 'Secretary of State for All-German Affairs' as 'Secretary of State for West German Affairs', Stoph saw fit to evoke, in the preamble of his draft for an intra-German

---

[165] For a typical statement reflecting these views, see Ulbricht's speech to the 17th SED Central Committee Plenum, *Neues Deutschland*, 28 Apr. 1965.

treaty, 'the interest for the future of the nation', in the name of which the two German states should regulate their relations through such an agreement.[166]

Similarly, the SED publicly corrected a statement by its chief propagandist Albert Norden which could be misinterpreted as suggesting that the GDR regarded the Federal Republic as a 'foreign' country: 'The GDR as the true representative of the German people's interests . . . does not regard West Germany as a foreign country (*Ausland*).'[167] Indeed, the SED's adherence to an all-German idea is clearly expressed in the new constitution of spring 1968 which speaks of the GDR as 'the Socialist State of the German Nation', an expression reminiscent of the historic 'Holy Roman Empire of the German Nation'.

The structure of the German division and trends in the international environment provide two additional conditions which promise to keep the German division on the agenda of problems to be solved. One is Berlin, which interlocks the two régimes. The city constantly forces the two parts of Germany to deal with each other and to seek some sort of accommodation which, in the last analysis, is impossible without regulating their relationship in a more harmonious manner. Similarly, the attempts in the international environment to lower East–West tensions and to overcome Europe's division contain an inbuilt incentive to deal with the German problem at the centre of the continent.

But the incentives to overcome Germany's division clash with the formidable array of obstacles which we have examined throughout the study. Reduced to its shortest formula, the situation can be summed up as follows: Germany's partition is an essential structural element of the present international system of muted bipolarity, though its relative stability is constantly threatened by the division itself. Some form of German unity is conceivable only as a result of major changes either within the present international system—but then in the form of major disruption and conflict—or of the international system itself—but then with no certainty of long-term stability. West Germany's conclusion has been similar to that of most other

---

[166] See Stoph's message to Kiesinger of 18 Sept. 1967, cited in n. 137.
[167] See *Neues Deutschland*, 19 and 20 Dec. 1967.

Western countries: namely, to live and to work with the paradox which makes acceptance of the *status quo* in Germany and Europe a precondition for its eventual change.

The Federal Republic now shares with other Western countries the belief that German unity can only be achieved within the larger process of overcoming the division of Europe. But the meaning of this process remains unclear and differs according to every author who has put forward proposals and views on the issue. To de Gaulle a reunited Europe implies that 'Russia must evolve in such a way that it sees its future, not through totalitarian constraints imposed on its own lands and on others, but through progress accomplished in common by free men and peoples. The nations which it has satellized must be able to play their role in a renewed Europe.'[168] In Strauss's 'Grand Design' a reunited Europe presupposes that Western Europe must establish itself as a grouping independent from the United States and the Soviet Union, and able to attract Eastern European countries. To spokesmen of the British and German left and the Great Coalition such a Europe requires an overhaul of the present alliances and the establishment of a new security system.

The lack of precise concepts, clear vision, and a Western consensus on such a new Europe alone rule out for the near future any *concrete* results on the desired rapprochement between the two parts of the divided continent beyond an increase in tourism, trade, or cultural exchange. But, more important, the sweeping nature of the necessary changes require enormous efforts, numerous international conferences and, above all, time to make possible progress towards a European reunification.

West Germany's attempt at adapting to protracted partition is therefore not a matter of choice but of necessity. As we have seen, the trend is clearly in the direction of accepting East Germany *de facto* as a second German state. But how far recognition of the division can proceed remains uncertain. German policy-makers have drawn a line beyond which recognition of East Germany is not supposed to go: the GDR cannot be regarded or treated as *Ausland*.[169] But even such a concept is

---

[168] See his press conference of 4 Feb. 1965, cited in n. 111.
[169] See Willy Brandt's interview in *Der Stern*, 23 Oct. 1967.

more of a declaration of faith in eventual German unity than a guide to practical action. West German leaders are unwilling to recognize the GDR *de jure* as a separate German state and to extend to it the formal paraphernalia of official relations between nations such as the exchange of ambassadors. But France and Austria are *Ausland*, and most German politicians would probably welcome it as great progress if the Federal Republic's relations with the GDR were as intensive and friendly as with these two 'foreign' countries in Western Europe.

To some Germans such as W. W. Schütz, Chairman of the 'Council for an Indivisible Germany', who caused considerable controversy with his proposals in December 1967, the answer lies in history.[170] The German Reich used to consist of different states which sometimes enjoyed considerable autonomy and which differed significantly in their internal structure. 'Recognition' was simply not a relevant problem in their internal relations, since they formed part of a larger confederal entity. In the same way Schütz proposes that the present two German states can have legal and official relations without the question of 'recognition' arising.

West Germany's increasing acceptance of the GDR, and dealings between the two régimes do not *solve* the German problem. Though a good case can be made for Bonn's new policy of establishing peaceful intra-German relations and of attempting to liberalize the East German régime, the new course, as we have seen, inevitably strains domestic politics and exposes the Federal Republic to risks and dangers from outside. Nor will the acceptance of the GDR eliminate those factors inherent in the German division which amplify tensions. Moreover, the active forces which preclude acceptance of the *status quo* as a solution to the German problem, such as domestic pressure for reunification in West Germany, the need to find a viable role for Berlin, or the pressure for *détente* in Europe, are unlikely to subside soon. Nevertheless the possibility cannot be entirely excluded that as a result of a *long* period of separation and of the moulding influence of two utterly different

---

[170] The memorandum and ensuing debate is published in Wilhelm Wolfgang Schütz, *Deutschlandmemorandum: Eine Denkschrift und Ihre Folgen* (1968).

political régimes and interests, two different German-speaking nations emerge.[171]

But West Germany's adaptation to the division and her attempt to enter into a peaceful working relationship with East Germany, though not a solution to the German problem, may still be a net gain. There are no *feasible* alternatives. Both a policy of hostility and isolation *vis-à-vis* the GDR, and a policy of short-cuts to unity, through threats, a deal with Moscow, etc., are counterproductive or dangerous and disruptive. Partly *because* of all the potentially destabilizing elements in a German division, which is going to last for a considerable length of time, a peaceful, if not co-operative relationship between the two parts of Germany may be desirable for the sake of stability in Europe and Germany. The least that can be said for such a course is that it helps to gain time. For Europe's old structural problem of how to accommodate the Germans and of creating a stable European order remains unsolved. More important, such a solution cannot and must not be based on the nation-state which, though it obstinately survives, has been rendered obsolete by the disasters of the past, the technological evolution and trans-national interaction of today, and the demands of tomorrow.

[171] See Waldemar Besson, 'Provokation des Selbstverständlichen', *Die Zeit*, 14 July 1967.

BIBLIOGRAPHY

Adenauer, Konrad. *Erinnerungen, 1945–53, 1953–5, 1955–9.* Stuttgart, 1965–7.

Allemann, Fritz René. *Zwischen Stabilität und Krise: Etappen der deutschen Politik 1955–63.* Munich, 1963.

Altmann, Rüdiger. *Das deutsche Risiko: Aussenpolitische Perspektiven.* Stuttgart, 1962.

Apel, Hans. *Spaltung: Deutschland zwischen Vernunft und Vernichtung.* Berlin, 1966.

Aron, Raymond. 'Is the European Idea Dying?' *Atlantic Community Quarterly,* V/1 (1967).

Auswärtiges Amt. *Die Bemühungen der deutschen Regierung und ihrer Verbündeten um die Einheit Deutschlands: 1955–66.* Bonn, 1966.

Bailey, George. 'East Germany: The Plan Collapses', *The Reporter,* 20 Apr. 1967.

Baring, Arnulf. *Der 17. Juni 1953.* Cologne, 1965.

——'Die westdeutsche Aussenpolitik der Ära Adenauer', *Politische Vierteljahresschrift,* IX/1 (1968).

Barzel, Rainer. *Gesichtspunkte eines Deutschen.* Düsseldorf, 1968.

Bender, Peter. *Offensive Entspannung: Möglichkeit für Deutschland.* Cologne, 1964.

Bensberger Kreis. *Ein Memorandum deutscher Katholiken zu den polnisch-deutschen Fragen.* Mainz, 1968.

Bergh, Godfried van Benthem van den. 'Contemporary Nationalism in the Western World', *Daedalus* (Summer 1966).

Bergstraesser, Arnold. 'Geschichtliches Bewusstsein und politische Entscheidung', in Waldemar Besson, ed., *Geschichte und Gegenwartsbewusstsein: Festschrift für Hans Rothfels.* Göttingen, 1963.

Besson, Waldemar. 'Prinzipienfragen der westdeutschen Aussenpolitik', *Politische Vierteljahresschrift,* IX/1 (1968).

Birnbaum, Immanuel. *Entzweite Nachbarn: Deutsche Politik in Osteuropa.* Frankfurt, 1968.

Birnbaum, Karl. 'The Western Alliance and European Security.' Cambridge, Mass., 1968, mimeo.

Birrenbach, Kurt. *Die Zukunft der atlantischen Gemeinschaft.* Freiburg, 1962.

Bluhm, Georg. *Die Oder-Neisse-Linie in der deutschen Aussenpolitik.* Freiburg, 1963.

Bowie, Robert. *Shaping the Future: Foreign Policy in an Age of Transition.* New York, 1964.

—— 'Tensions within the Alliance', *Foreign Affairs*, XLII/1 (1963).

Bracher, Karl Dietrich. *Deutschland zwischen Demokratie und Diktatur.* Bern, 1964.

—— 'Wird Bonn doch Weimar?' *Der Spiegel*, 13 Mar. 1967.

Brandt, Willy. 'Entspannungspolitik mit langem Atem', *Aussenpolitik*, XVIII/8 (1967).

—— 'German Policy Toward the East', *Foreign Affairs*, XLVI/3 (1968).

—— *The Ordeal of Coexistence.* Cambridge, Mass., 1963.

Brzezinski, Zbigniew. *Alternative to Partition: For a Broader Conception of America's Role in Europe.* New York, 1965.

—— and William E. Griffith. 'Peaceful Engagement in Eastern Europe', *Foreign Affairs*, XXXIX/4 (1961).

Camps, Miriam. *European Unification in the Sixties, from the Veto to the Crisis.* London, OUP, 1967.

Conze, Werner. *Das deutsch-russische Verhältnis im Wandel der modernen Welt.* Göttingen, 1967.

Cornides, Wilhelm. 'Prioritäten des Friedens in Europa', *Europa-Archiv*, XX/1 (1965), XXI/3 (1966).

Croan, Melvin. 'Eastern Policy and the Dilemmas of Germany's Division.' Cambridge, Mass., 1965, mimeo (unpubl.).

Dahrendorf, Ralf. *Society and Democracy in Germany.* Garden City, 1967.

Deuerlein, Ernst. *Deutschland wie Chruschtschow es will.* Bonn, 1961.

Deutsch, Karl. W. and Lewis J. Edinger. 'Foreign Policy of the German Federal Republic', in Roy Macridis, ed., *Foreign Policy in World Politics.* 3rd ed., Englewood Cliffs, 1966.

—— *Germany Rejoins the Powers.* London, OUP, 1959.

Domes, Alfred, ed. *Die Politik des Westens und Osteuropa.* Cologne, 1966.

Dönhoff, Marion Gräfin, Rudolf Walter Leonhardt, and Theo Sommer. *Reise in ein fernes Land: Bericht über Kultur, Wirtschaft und Politik in der DDR.* Hamburg, 1964.

Eberlein, Ludwig. *Experiment Berlin: Plädoyer für eine deutsche Konföderation.* Cologne, 1967.

Epstein, Klaus. 'The Adenauer Era in German History', in Stephen R. Graubard, ed., *A New Europe?* Boston, 1964.

Erdmenger, Klaus. *Das folgenschwere Missverständnis: Bonn und die sowjetische Deutschlandpolitik 1949–55.* Freiburg, 1967.

Erler, Fritz. *Democracy in Germany.* Cambridge, Mass., 1965.

Erler, Fritz. 'The Basis of Partnership', *Foreign Affairs*, XLII/1 (1963).

Eschenburg, Theodor. *Die deutsche Frage: Verfassungsprobleme der Wiedervereinigung*. Munich, 1959.

Feld, Werner. *Reunification and West German–Soviet Relations*. The Hague, 1963.

Fijalkowsky, Jürgen *et al*. *Berlin—Hauptstadtanspruch und Westintegration*. Cologne, 1967.

Fontaine, André. *Histoire de la guerre froide, 1917–50*. Paris, 1965. *1950–67*. Paris, 1967.

Freund, Gerald. *Germany between Two Worlds*. New York, 1961.

Gaus, Günter. *Staatserhaltende Opposition oder Hat die SPD kapituliert? Gespräche mit Herbert Wehner*. Reinbek/bei Hamburg, 1966.

Grewe, Wilhelm G. *Deutsche Aussenpolitik der Nachkriegszeit*. Stuttgart, 1960.

Griffith, William E. 'Die Vereinigten Staaten und die Sowjetunion in Europa: Rüstungswettlauf, Technologie, Deutschlandproblem', *Neue Welt*, VIII/4 (1967).

—— 'German Problems and American Policies.' Cambridge, Mass., 1965, mimeo.

Grosser, Alfred. *Die Bonner Demokratie*. Düsseldorf, 1960.

—— *Die Bundesrepublik Deutschland: Bilanz einer Entwicklung*. Tübingen, 1967.

—— *French Foreign Policy under de Gaulle*. Boston, 1967.

—— *La Quatrième République et sa politique extérieure*. Paris, 1961.

—— 'France and Germany: Divergent Outlooks', *Foreign Affairs*, XLIV/1 (1965).

Guttenberg, Karl Theodor Freiherr zu. *Wenn der Westen will: Plädoyer für eine mutige Politik*. 2nd ed. Stuttgart, 1965.

Haas, Ernst B. 'Technocracy, Pluralism, and the New Europe', in Stephen R. Graubard ed. *A New Europe?* Boston, 1964.

Haffner, Sebastian. 'The Berlin Crisis', *Survey*, no. 44/45 (1962).

Hangen, Welles. *The Muted Revolution. East Germany's Challenge to Russia and the West*. New York, 1966.

Hanrieder, Wolfram F. *West German Foreign Policy: 1949–63*. Stanford, 1967.

Hartmann, Frederick H. *Germany between East and West: The Reunification Problem*. Englewood Cliffs, 1965.

Hassner, Pierre. 'Change and Security in Europe: pt 1: The Background', *Adelphi Paper*, no. 45, London, 1968.

—— 'German and European Unification: Two Problems or One?', *Survey*, no. 61 (1966).

—— and John Newhouse. *Diplomacy in the West: Out from Paradox.* New York, 1966.

Heinemann, Gustav. *Verfehlte Deutschlandpolitik: Irreführung und Selbsttäuschung.* Frankfurt, 1966.

Henkys, Reinhard, ed. *Deutschland und die östlichen Nachbarn.* Stuttgart, 1966.

Hoffmann, Stanley. 'De Gaulle, Europe, and the Atlantic Alliance', *Internat. Organization,* XVIII/1 (1964).

—— *Gulliver's Troubles, or the Setting of American Foreign Policy.* New York, 1968.

—— 'Obstinate or Obsolete? The Fate of the Nation and the Case of Western Europe', *Daedalus* (Summer 1966).

Hubatsch, Walther, ed., *Die deutsche Frage.* 2nd ed. Würzburg, 1964.

Jäckel, Hartmut. 'Kontakte ohne Anerkennung? Der Briefwechsel Kiesinger-Stoph.' *Der Monat,* no. 235 (1968).

Jacobsen, Hans Adolf and Otto Stenzl, eds. *Deutschland und die Welt: Zur Aussenpolitik der Bundesrepublik 1949–63.* Munich, 1964.

Jaksch, Wenzel. *Westeuropa–Osteuropa–Sowjetunion: Perspektiven wirtschaftlicher Zusammenarbeit.* Bonn, 1965.

Jaspers, Karl. *Lebensfragen der deutschen Politik.* Munich, 1963.

—— *Wohin treibt die Bundesrepublik: Tatsachen—Gefahren—Chancen.* Munich, 1966.

Jouve, Edmond. *Le Général de Gaulle et la construction de l'Europe: 1940–66.* 2 vols. Paris, 1967.

Kaiser, Karl. 'Die neue Abhängigkeit der atlantischen Staaten', *Europa-Archiv,* XVII/23 (1962).

—— 'Die amerikanische Aussenpolitik im Wandel: Die Vereinigten Staaten und Westeuropa in der westlichen Allianz.' *Europa-Archiv,* XIX/24 (1964).

—— 'Die deutsche Frage', *Frankfurter Hefte,* XX/11 & 12 (1965), XXI/1 (1966).

—— *EWG und Freihandelszone: England und der Kontinent in der europäischen Integration.* Leyden, 1963.

—— 'The US and the EEC in the Atlantic System: The Problem of Theory', *J. Common Market Studies,* V/4 (1967).

Kissinger, Henry A. 'For a New Atlantic Alliance', *The Reporter,* 14 July 1966.

—— *The Necessity for Choice: Prospects of American Foreign Policy.* Garden City, 1961.

—— *The Troubled Partnership: A Reappraisal of the Atlantic Alliance.* New York, 1965.

Kogon, Eugen. *Die unvollendete Erneuerung: Deutschland im Kräftefeld, 1945–63.* Frankfurt, 1964.

Kopp, Fritz. *Kurs auf ganz Deutschland? Die Deutschlandpolitik der S.E.D.* Stuttgart, 1965.

Krengel, Rolf. *Die Bedeutung des Ost-West-Handels für die Ost-West-Beziehungen.* Göttingen, 1967.

Kuby, Heinz. *Provokation Europa: Die Bedingungen seines politischen Überlebens.* Cologne, 1965.

Lindberg, Leon N. 'Integration as a Source of Stress on the European Community System.' *Internat. Organization,* XX/1 (1966).

Löwenthal, Richard. 'Der Einfluss Chinas auf die Entwicklung des Ost-West-Konflikts in Europa.' *Europa-Archiv,* XXII/10 (1967).

—— 'Problems of Contemporary Germany' (provisional title). Paper delivered to the German Research Program of Harvard University, Mar. 1968, forthcoming.

—— 'The Germans feel like Germans again', *New York Times Magazine,* 21 Nov. 1965.

Löwenthal, Richard, ed. *Ist der Osten noch ein Block?* Stuttgart, 1967.

Ludz, Peter Christian. *Parteielite im Wandel: Funktionsaufbau, Sozialstruktur und Ideologie der SED-Führung.* Cologne, 1967.

—— ed. 'Studien und Materialien zur Soziologie der DDR', *Kölner Zeitschrift für Soziologie und Sozialpsychologie,* Special issue no. 8 (1964).

Majonica, Ernst. *Deutsche Aussenpolitik.* Stuttgart, 1965.

Mander, John. *Berlin, Hostage for the West.* London, 1962.

Mann, Golo. *Verzicht oder Forderung? Die deutschen Ostgrenzen.* Freiburg, 1964.

Markert, Werner, ed. *Deutsch-russische Beziehungen von Bismarck bis zur Gegenwart.* Stuttgart, 1964.

Meissner, Boris. *Russland, die Westmächte und Deutschland; Die sowjetische Deutschlandpolitik, 1943–53.* Hamburg, 1953.

Merkl, Peter H. *The Origin of the West German Republic.* London, OUP, 1963.

Morgan, Roger. 'The Scope of German Foreign Policy', *Yearbook of World Affairs, 1966.* London, 1966.

Newhouse, John. *Collision in Brussels: The Common Market Crisis of 30 June 1965.* New York, 1967.

Planck, Charles R. *The Changing Status of German Reunification in Western Diplomacy: 1955–66.* Baltimore, 1967.

Pritzel, Konstantin. *Die wirtschaftliche Integration der sowjetischen Besatzungszone Deutschlands in den Ostblock und ihre politischen Aspekte.* Bonn, 1965.

Raiser, Ludwig. 'Deutsche Ostpolitik im Lichte der Denkschrift der evangelischen Kirche', *Europa-Archiv*, XXI/6 (1966).

Reuther, Helmut, ed. *Deutschlands Aussenpolitik seit 1955*. Stuttgart, 1965.

Reynaud, Paul. *The Foreign Policy of Charles de Gaulle*. London, 1964.

Richardson, James L. *Germany and the Atlantic Alliance: The Interaction of Strategy and Politics*. London, OUP, 1966.

Richert, Ernst. *Das Zweite Deutschland: Ein Staat der nicht sein darf*. Gütersloh, 1964.

Roegele, Otto B. *Versöhnung oder Hass? Der Briefwechsel der Bischöfe Polens und Deutschlands und seine Folgen*. Osnabrück, 1966.

Ruhm von Oppen, Beate, ed. *Documents on Germany under Occupation, 1945-54*. London, OUP, 1958.

Russett, Bruce M. and Carolyn C. Cooper. 'Arms Control in Europe: Proposals and Political Constraints.' Denver (Col), 1967, mimeo.

Saeter, Martin. *Okkupation, Integration, Gleichberechtigung*. Oslo, 1967.

Scheuch, Erwin. *Politische Strukturen der Bundesrepublik*. Munich, 1968.

Schmidt, Helmut. 'Deutschlandpolitik unter den sich ändernden weltpolitischen Bedingungen', *Tatsachen-Argumente*, no. 205 (1966).

Schmitt, Walter E. *Krieg in Deutschland: Strategie und Taktik der sowjet-russischen Deutschlandpolitik seit 1945*. Düsseldorf, 1961.

Schollwer, Wolfgang. *Deutschland- und Aussenpolitik*. Frankfurt, 1967.

Schröder, Gerhard. 'Germany looks at Eastern Europe', *Foreign Affairs*, XLIV/1 (1965).

Schulz, Eberhard. *An Ulbricht führt kein Weg mehr vorbei: Provozierende Thesen zur deutschen Frage*. Hamburg, 1967.

Schulz, Hans-Dieter. 'Moskaus wichtigster Partner: Die Stellung der "DDR" im Ostblock', *Europa-Archiv*, XIX/21 (1964).

Schütz, Wilhelm Wolfgang. *Deutschland-Memorandum: Eine Denkschrift und ihre Folgen*. Frankfurt, 1968.

—— *Modelle der Deutschlandpolitik: Wege zu einer neuen Aussenpolitik*. Cologne, 1966.

—— *Reform der Deutschlandpolitik*. Cologne, 1966.

Schwarz, Hans-Peter. *Vom Reich zur Bundesrepublik. Deutschland im Widerstreit der aussenpolitischen Konzeption in den Jahren der Besatzungsherrschaft 1945-9*. Neuwied, 1966.

Schwoebel, Jean. *Les deux K., Berlin et la paix*. Paris, 1963.

Sethe, Paul. *Öffnung nach Osten: Weltpolitische Realitäten zwischen Bonn, Paris und Moskau*. Frankfurt, 1966.

Shell, Kurt L. *Bedrohung und Bewährung: Führung und Bevölkerung in der Berliner Krise*. Cologne, 1966.

Siegler, Heinrich von. *Kennedy oder de Gaulle? Probleme der Atlantik- und Europapolitik.* Bonn, 1963.

—— *Wiedervereinigung und Sicherheit Deutschlands.* 5th ed. Bonn, 1964.

—— *Dokumentation zur Deutschlandfrage: 1961–5.* Bonn, 1966.

Smith, Jean E. *The Defense of Berlin.* Baltimore, 1963.

—— 'The Red Prussianism of the German Democratic Republic', *Political Science Quarterly*, LXXXII/3 (1967).

Sommer, Theo. 'Bonn Changes Course', *Foreign Affairs*, XLV/3 (1967).

Sommer, Theo, ed. *Denken an Deutschland: Zum Problem der Wiedervereinigung.* Hamburg, 1966.

S.P.D. *Bestandsaufnahme 1966: Eine Dokumentation.* Bonn, 1966.

Speier, Hans. *Divided Berlin: The Anatomy of Soviet Political Blackmail.* New York, 1961.

Stehle, Hansjakob. *Nachbar Polen.* Rev. ed. Frankfurt, 1968.

Stern, Carola. 'East Germany', in William E. Griffith, ed., *Communism in Europe*, ii. Cambridge, Mass., 1966.

—— *Ulbricht: Eine politische Biographie.* Cologne, 1963.

Stimmen zur Denkschrift der EKD. Cologne, 1966.

Stöcker, Hans A. 'Völkerrechtliche Implikationen des Heimatrechts', *Europa-Archiv*, XXI/15 (1966).

Stolper, Wolfgang F. *The Structure of the East German Economy.* Cambridge, Mass., 1960.

Storbeck, Dietrich. *Berlin: Bestand und Möglichkeiten.* Cologne, 1964.

Strauss, Franz Josef. *The Grand Design: A European Solution to German Reunification.* London, 1965.

Studnitz, Hans-Georg von. *Bismarck in Bonn: Bemerkungen zur Aussenpolitik.* Stuttgart, 1964.

Tudyka, Kurt P. 'Die DDR im Kräftefeld des Ost-West-Konflikts', *Europa-Archiv*, XXI/1 (1966).

—— ed. *Das geteilte Deutschland.* Stuttgart, 1965.

Váli, Ferenc A. *The Quest for a United Germany.* Baltimore, 1967.

Vetter, Gottfried. 'Passierscheine in Deutschland', *Europa-Archiv*, XIX/9 (1964).

Watt, D. C. *Britain looks to Germany: British Opinion and Policy towards Germany since 1945.* London, 1965.

Weizsäcker, Carl Friedrich Freiherr von. 'Über weltpolitische Prognosen', *Europa-Archiv*, XXI/1 (1966).

Wettig, Gerhard. *Entmilitarisierung und Wiederbewaffnung Deutschlands.* Munich, 1967.

Wettig, Gerhard. 'The SED—SPD Dialogue: Communist Political Strategy', *Orbis*, XI/2 (1967).

Wildenmann, Rudolf. *Macht und Konsens als Problem der Innen- und Aussenpolitik.* Frankfurt, 1963.

Wilkens, Erwin, ed. *Vertreibung und Versöhnung: Die Synode der EKD zur Denkschrift.* Stuttgart, 1966.

Willis, F. Roy. *France, Germany, and the New Europe, 1965-7.* Rev. ed. London, OUP, 1968.

Windsor, Philip. *City on Leave: A History of Berlin 1945–62.* New York, 1963.

Wolfe, James. *Indivisible Germany: Illusion or Reality?* The Hague, 1963.

Younger, Kenneth. *Changing Perspectives in British Foreign Policy.* London, OUP, 1964.

PUBLICATIONS WRITTEN UNDER THE AUSPICES OF THE
CENTER FOR INTERNATIONAL AFFAIRS
HARVARD UNIVERSITY

Books

The Soviet Bloc, by Zbigniew K. Brzezinski (jointly with the Russian Research Center), 1960. Harvard University Press.

The Necessity for Choice, by Henry A. Kissinger, 1961. Harper & Bros.

Strategy and Arms Control, by Thomas C. Schelling and Morton H. Halperin, 1961. Twentieth Century Fund.

Rift and Revolt in Hungary, by Ferenc A. Váli, 1961. Harvard Univeristy Press.

United States Manufacturing Investment in Brazil, by Lincoln Gordon and Engelbert L. Grommers, 1962. Harvard Business School.

The Economy of Cyprus, by A. J. Meyer, with Simos Vassiliou (jointly with the Center for Middle Eastern Studies), 1962. Harvard University Press.

Entrepreneurs of Lebanon, by Yusif A. Sayigh (jointly with the Center for Middle Eastern Studies), 1962. Harvard University Press.

Communist China 1955–1959: Policy Documents with Analysis, with a Foreword by Robert R. Bowie and John K. Fairbank (jointly with the East Asian Research Center), 1962. Harvard University Press.

In Search of France, by Stanley Hoffmann, Charles P. Kindleberger, Laurence Wylie, Jesse R. Pitts, Jean-Baptiste Duroselle, and François Goguel, 1963. Harvard University Press.

Somali Nationalism, by Saadia Touval, 1963. Harvard University Press.

The Dilemma of Mexico's Development, by Raymond Vernon, 1963. Harvard University Press.

Limited War in the Nuclear Age, by Morton H. Halperin, 1963. John Wiley & Sons.

The Arms Debate, by Robert A. Levine, 1963. Harvard University Press.

Africans on the Land, by Montague Yudelman, 1964. Harvard University Press.

Counterinsurgency Warfare, by David Galula, 1964. Frederick A. Praeger, Inc.

People and Policy in the Middle East, by Max Weston Thornburg, 1964. W. W. Norton & Co.

Shaping the Future, by Robert R. Bowie, 1964. Columbia University Press.

Foreign Aid and Foreign Policy, by Edward S. Mason (jointly with the Council on Foreign Relations), 1964. Harper & Row.

Public Policy and Private Enterprise in Mexico, by M. S. Wionczek, D. H. Shelton, C. P. Blair, and R. Izquierdo, ed. Raymond Vernon, 1964. Harvard University Press.

How Nations Negotiate, by Fred C. Iklé, 1964. Harper & Row.

China and the Bomb, by Morton H. Halperin (jointly with the East Asian Research Center), 1965. Frederick A. Praeger, Inc.

Democracy in Germany, by Fritz Erler (Jodidi Lectures), 1965. Harvard University Press.

The Troubled Partnership, by Henry A. Kissinger (jointly with the Council on Foreign Relations), 1965. McGraw-Hill Book Co.

The Rise of Nationalism in Central Africa, by Robert I. Rotberg, 1965. Harvard University Press.

Pan-Africanism and East African Integration, by Joseph S. Nye, Jr., 1965. Harvard University Press.

Communist China and Arms Control, by Morton H. Halperin and Dwight H. Perkins (jointly with the East Asian Research Center), 1965. Frederick A. Praeger, Inc.

Problems of National Strategy, ed. Henry Kissinger, 1965. Frederick A. Praeger, Inc.

Deterrence before Hiroshima: The Airpower Background of Modern Strategy, by George H. Quester, 1966. John Wiley & Sons.

Containing the Arms Race, by Jeremy J. Stone, 1966. M.I.T. Press.

Germany and the Atlantic Alliance: The Interaction of Strategy and Politics, by James L. Richardson, 1966. Harvard Universsity Press.

Arms and Influence, by Thomas C. Schelling, 1966. Yale University Press.

Planning without Facts, by Wolfgang Stolper, 1966. Harvard University Press.

Political Change in a West African State, by Martin L. Kilson, 1966. Harvard Univeristy Press.

Export Instability and Economic Development, by Alasdair MacBean, 1966. Harvard University Press.

Foreign Policy and Democratic Politics, by Kenneth N. Waltz (jointly with the Institute of War and Peace Studies, Columbia University), 1967. Little, Brown & Co.

Contemporary Military Strategy, by Morton H. Halperin, 1967. Little, Brown.

Sino-Soviet Relations and Arms Control, ed. Morton H. Halperin (jointly with the East Asian Research Center), 1967. M.I.T. Press.

Africa and United States Policy, by Rupert Emerson, 1967. Prentice-Hall.

Elites in Latin America, ed. S. M. Lipset and Aldo Solari, 1967. Oxford University Press.

Europe's Postwar Growth, by Charles P. Kindleberger, 1967. Harvard University Press.

The Rise and Decline of the Cold War, by Paul Seabury, 1967. Basic Books.

Student Politics, ed. Seymour Martin Lipset, 1967. Basic Books.

Pakistan's Development: Social Goals and Private Incentives, by Gustav F. Papanek, 1967. Harvard University Press.

Strike a Blow and Die: A Narrative of Race Relations in Colonial Africa, by George Simeon Mwase. Edited and introduced by Robert T. Rotberg, 1967. Harvard University Press.

Aid, Influence, and Foreign Policy, by Joan M. Nelson, 1968. Macmillan.

International Regionalism, by Joseph S. Nye, 1968. Little, Brown.

The TFX Decision: McNamara and the Military, by Robert J. Art, 1968. Little, Brown.

Korea: The Politics of the Vortex, by Gregory Henderson, 1968. Harvard University Press.

Political Development in Latin America, by Martin Needler, 1968. Random House.

Revolution and Counterrevolution: Change and Persistence in Social Structures, by Seymour Martin Lipset, 1968. Basic Books.

Agrarian Socialism, by Seymour Martin Lipset, rev. ed., 1968. Doubleday-Anchor Books.

The Precarious Republic, by Michael C. Hudson, 1968. Random House.

German Foreign Policy in Transition: Bonn between East and West, by Karl Kaiser, 1968. Oxford University Press.

OCCASIONAL PAPERS PUBLISHED BY THE CENTER FOR INTERNATIONAL AFFAIRS

1. *A Plan for Planning: The Need for a Better Method of Assisting Underdeveloped Countries on Their Economic Policies*, by Gustav F. Papanek, 1961. Out of print.

2. *The Flow of Resources from Rich to Poor*, by Alan D. Neale, 1961.

3. *Limited War: An Essay on the Development of the Theory and an Annotated Bibliography*, by Morton H. Halperin, 1962. Out of print.

4. *Reflections on the Failure of the First West Indian Federation*, by Hugh W. Springer, 1962. Out of print.

5. *On the Interaction of Opposing Forces under Possible Arms Agreements,* by Glenn A. Kent, 1963.
6. *Europe's Northern Cap and the Soviet Union,* by Nils Örvik, 1963.
7. *Civil Administration in the Punjab: An Analysis of a State Government in India,* by E. N. Mangat Rai, 1963.
8. *On the Appropriate Size of a Development Program,* by Edward S. Mason, 1964.
9. *Self-Determination Revisited in the Era of Decolonization,* by Rupert Emerson, 1964.
10. *The Planning and Execution of Economic Development in Southeast Asia,* by Clair Wilcox, 1965.
11. *Pan-Africanism in Action,* by Albert Tevoedjre, 1965.
12. *Is China Turning In?* by Morton H. Halperin, 1965.
13. *Economic Development in India and Pakistan,* by Edward S. Mason, 1966.
14. *The Role of the Military in Recent Turkish Politics,* by Ergun Özbudun, 1966.
15. *Economic Development and Individual Change: A Social-Psychological Study of the Comilla Experiment in Pakistan,* by Howard Schuman, 1967.
16. *A Select Bibliography on Students, Politics, and Higher Education,* by Philip G. Altbach, 1967.
17. *Europe's Political Puzzle: A Study of the Fouchet Negotiations and the 1963 Veto,* by Alessandro Silj, 1967.
18. *The Cap and the Straits: Problems of Nordic Security,* by Jan Klenberg, 1968.
19. *Cyprus: The Law and Politics of Civil Strife,* by Linda B. Miller, 1968.

INDEX*

---

* For works cited in footnotes, see Bibliography.